In the beginning

was the Word

and so shall it be again,

and the Word

is the Law,

and the Law

is Love.

A Leaders of the Way book

From the same publisher:

The Way of Love
Joseph of Arimathea Tells the True
Story behind the Message of Christ
Compiled by Peter Wheeler
ISBN 90-75635-01-X. 256pp
(Also available in Dutch)

The Memories of Josephes
Soul Memories of a Cousin of Jesus
David Davidson
ISBN 0-9532007-0-1. 256pp

The Children of Light
Father Abraham on the
Fulfilment of a Prophecy
Compiled by David Davidson
ISBN 0-9532007-4-4. 96pp
(Monograph)

In preparation:

The Way of Truth
Compiled by Graham Timmins

The Way of Stones
Compiled by Zanne Findlay

The Way of Diet and Health
Compiled by Rosalind Pencherek

THE WAY
OF SOUL
Part 1

Compiled by David Davidson

Series Editor: Peter Wheeler
Copy Editors: Carlen Pierce and Judith Timmins
Research: Anthony Felt
Transcription: Elizabeth Price
Editorial Panel: All the above with
Zanne Findlay and Josef Schmied
Cover Design: David Davidson

Published by The Leaders Partnership,
PO box 16457, London, SE14 5WH, UK.
ISBN 0-9532007-4-4

First edition 1999. Printed in the UK
by Redwood Books, Trowbridge, Wiltshire
Set in 11 on 14 point Galliard

The Way of Soul

The Monograph Series

The Arimathean Foundation has been established to promote and distribute the spiritual teachings of Joseph of Arimathea, Father Abraham and the Prophet Elijah, who currently speak through a deep-trance channel.

Our first publication, 'The Way of Love,' is a biography of Joseph of Arimathea told through a mosaic of discussions he has had with individuals about past lives they lived during the time of Christ. Through these verbatim accounts he reveals the story of his family, the events surrounding his life and those of his nephew Yeshua, who was to become the Christ.

The second book, 'The Memories of Josephes,' is an intimate account of the life of the elder son of the Arimathean and his relationship with Yeshua. As children they were cousins and playmates; as adults Josephes was the companion and confidant of Yeshua. This inspired account is made up of vivid descriptions and pictures that clearly portray the mood of the time.

'The Way of Truth' is an exposé of the enduring truth that lies behind some of the most perplexing scientific and spiritual riddles facing humanity today.

In addition to these major works, this series of smaller publications, 'the Monographs,' has been established so that talks on specific and topical subjects from the three spiritual teachers, as well as inspired writings from the Arimathean Group, can be placed before the public.

The first in the Monograph series was on the Children of Light. This publication comprises the contents of five hour-long discussions with Father Abraham, who is the spiritual leader of these children. He has set out the needs, purpose and vision of a generation of very old souls who, with our help and encouragement, will restore balance, harmony and spiritual understanding to a world that is teetering on the edge of disaster.

In this, the second of the Monographs, this time based on six talks, Joseph of Arimathea presents a major thesis on soul: what it is, where it comes from, its relationship to God and to humanity, the vital importance of soul in this age and most importantly the pathway of soul, known since the beginning of time as 'The Way.'

Introduction

These words are collated from transcripts of tape recordings of a deep-trance, direct-voice channel* who wishes to remain anonymous. Now in her late sixties, she started her channelling over twenty years ago as many others do, through an attraction to the Spiritualist Church. She was guided by experienced mediums, sat in development circles and practised her talent through private and group consultations. As time went by and she became more adept one particular spiritual teacher began to speak through her regularly and then became her constant spiritual companion. The quality of his teaching was recognised as profound and as both he and she began to achieve recognition beyond Spiritualist circles, the channel built a following of people who came regularly to listen to the being who spoke through her and identified himself as 'the Master.'

About ten years ago the Master revealed that in a previous life he had been Joseph of Arimathea, uncle and guardian of Jesus (known to his family as Yeshua), and it was in his family tomb that the body of Christ was laid after the crucifixion. He also said that he was the spokesperson for a group of souls on the causal plane and that when he spoke through the channel he was speaking with the accumulated wisdom of many lives, some of them quite well-known. At about the same time he began to reveal to certain of the people who were regular visitors to the home of the channel that an aspect of their Higher Selves had also been incarnate at the time of Christ and had a connection with the events of his life. Much of the information he gave at that time has now been collated and published in 'The Way of Love,' compiled by Peter Wheeler.

In early 1993, in response to discussions with both the channel and the Master, one of those who had been identified by Joseph as having a role in the events surrounding Christ organised a reunion for all the others in a similar position. This formed the basis for what has now become a regular retreat for

*A deep-trance channel is one who is literally 'entranced' by the teachers who speak through them. It is a very particular talent that takes many years to develop; to be able voluntarily to surrender to unconsciousness so that a spiritual being can speak requires an extraordinary trust. In this case the channel knows nothing about what has passed between the teacher who speaks through her and those who are listening until she is told by the audience or hears a tape recording of the proceedings.

a group that numbers thirty-six. In one of these early meetings the second of a trinity of teachers was introduced through the channel; this was the Prophet Elijah. The following year a third teacher was introduced – Father Abraham of the old Testament. The work of these three Teachers, all of whom are directly connected to the Christ, and the group of thirty six that now surrounds them is primarily to do with earth-healing and spreading their words through the publication of books.

The Way of Soul
In this, the second book in the monograph series Joseph of Arimathea, who was the first and remains the most frequent speaker through our channel, has elected to speak on the pathway of the soul. As one of those who attended the series of talks personally and has subsequently been involved in preparing this book for publication I have been very aware of how much is lost once words are written down and printed. I wish you too could have been at the lectures personally, could have felt the change in atmosphere as Master Joseph entered his channel. I wish you could have seen our beloved channel stand up and in an entirely different voice utter the words that Joseph always uses to greet those who come to listen, 'My children, shalom...' You would have seen the most marvellous transformation as she started to speak, the way she turned her head and nodded, the pauses between words, the deep attention she gave to those who spoke to her, the way she held her hands as she talked. They were the gestures of a nobleman, the authority and gravity of a great teacher – teacher and counsellor, husband and father, a leader in the Sanhedrin who lived over two thousand years ago, now an ascended master. You would have heard for yourselves the cadence and power of his speech, sometimes tender, sometimes humorous, sometimes emphatic, sometimes enigmatic and always so filled with emotion when he talked of his life, his family and his beloved nephew, Yeshua.

You would have seen for yourselves how he taught the little group of fifteen or so people who gathered to listen through the winter months, how he carefully described and constructed from the foundations up a picture of the spiritual architecture that towers above humanity, architecture that has at its heart the soul, that peculiar thing which twinkles in the eyes of humanity and marks us out as belonging to God in a very special way. As he talked to us, always patient, ever loving, always willing to explain again, I often thought that he was being exactly what he taught, he was demonstrating soul, unencumbered by the travails of life. As you read his words I hope you will hold this image in your mind. Each reply he has given spawns a hundred more questions in its wake However for those of us present he answered an unasked question, not in words but directly, in his attitude. The answer was love.

Why now?

At the end of each age, approximately every two thousand years, a new archangel steps forward to oversee the development and learning of humanity. In the current transition Uriel, who represents the purple light, is moving on and Michael, who represents the gold, is coming into prominence. This is why the Aquarian age is often referred to as the Golden age. During the Piscean age the development and understanding of science was brought to a pinnacle and has provided humanity with power and wealth. However this scientific approach, the study of the particular, without being balanced by a deeper understanding of the spiritual, the understanding of the whole, has brought with it the seeds of its own destruction, seeds which are beginning to germinate across the planet. This is why Master Joseph, The Prophet Elijah and Father Abraham are channelling at this time. They are speaking to provide a focus for the Children of Light, spiritual elders in the bodies of children who are being born to help humanity through the changes needed to enter the Golden age. They are here to speak again the ancient wisdoms, those elegant truths of life that throughout history have always surfaced during the very darkest hours of humanity.

The Way of Soul Part Two

The Master has always maintained that his teaching is progressive, it builds slowly over time. For this reason he has asked that a second volume, 'The Way of Soul Part Two' be prepared. This book, due to be published in early 2000, is a chronological compilation of his teachings on soul over the last twenty years. Those who wish to gain a deeper understanding can follow the progression of the teachings step by step. The extracts in the questions and answers at the end of this book are taken from these earlier teachings.

David Davidson, Summer 1999

Chapter 1

Talk One, November

The work of the three spiritual teachers. The relationship of God, soul and personality. The relationship of soul and spirit. Creation and the big bang. The spirals of creation.

Master: My children, welcome. Shalom! It has been some time since we were made aware that this particular series of talks was envisioned in order to prepare a book which is entirely about the journey of the soul. It is one of those subjects very dear to our heart and all of the spiritual teachers from time to time have incorporated this particular subject within other talks that have been given. It is the kind of subject that can go on and on for a very long time, because the journey of the soul, from its very beginning until that time when it is no longer needed to take place universally, will cover many millions of years. Some of the basic details that we have given in the past will indeed be spoken of once more as we go through these six talks with you.

Try and put out of your minds what you have read in our transcripts of talks given before. We know it is hoped that when this book is produced it will be comprehensive. In a way many of these books will supplant the transcripts which you have been used to reading. As time moves forward, so also does the method of teaching. If everything remained the same, remained constantly even, there would be no encouragement for people to learn, to widen their horizons, to be aware and compare that of the past to what is happening at the moment and what will happen in the future.

Abraham and Elijah
As part of our need for the work that we have been engaged upon for several thousand years to progress, we had to start relatively quietly and slowly, building up as time passed and people's interest became greater to the true purpose of our work. When I use the collective word 'our,' it is not only those aspects within my Higher Self as that of Joseph, but also of course the other two Teachers who, from time to time, have come and spoken with you. We know that there are several present at this time who have not had the pleasure of speaking with either Father Abraham or Elijah. Whether they will decide to speak a little during this series of talks I cannot yet promise.

It is I myself, of course, who have been invited to do this, but they have their understandings, their knowledge, in the same way as I, Joseph, have and in the same way that your knowledge throughout the years has expanded and grown in your fields of endeavour, not always taking the same route, so it is with the three Teachers and myself. In order to start this talk in the proper manner, we need to understand that very basic detail as to exactly what soul is, what comprises soul. We are very aware that the great majority of you already know this, but just think of all those people who will be encouraged to buy these words and who will not know; therefore if we began in a more advanced way they would put down the book, they would say, 'But I don't really understand what is meant by soul. Is it the same as spirit, is it the same as the life force which enables me to have my being, or is it something to do with the mind, or even the brain?' We certainly hope that many people who have never had any particular interest in learning spiritual matters will pick up the book, turn the pages and be interested in the description of soul.

Soul and Spirit
The soul is the spiritual, living part of the personality. It is different from the spirit because the spirit is the God force which animates the soul into life, which gives it consciousness. Going back a few million years when the universe was first created, that universe was comprised of soul. Soul was that mass of energy that entailed an understanding of what life meant, but did not actually animate life. Soul at that time emanated from the Creative Force as part of this force. Soul therefore has been within the universe since the very beginning of time itself – time as man has come to know it, as that which goes steadfastly forward through night and through day.

Spirit came into being when that Creative Force linked with what you know as God – God being the intelligence that gives life to all things, from the minutest of microbes to the largest living land animal, which we believe is now the elephant, to all of man, to all the world of nature, the flowers and the trees – that living breath is God. So you might well say, 'If soul has existed since the beginning of all time and we understand that God created the universe, what is going wrong? Does this Teacher standing before us have his wires crossed, or does he truly know something we don't know about the creation?'

Your spiritual teachers are not all-knowing. We know a great deal, because once free of the body, once free of that commodity within man that must always seek reassurance, seek evidence for everything that is before him, that commodity that cannot accept the word of another unless it is proved, we have an inner knowing because of the direct link through our souls, released from the body, with God.

God is indeed an energy, a very powerful energy, but God is not soul, God is spirit. So what has been around since the beginning of time and what was the beginning of time, when was this? Within your statutory prayers there are the words 'world without end.' Part of the prayer also refers to 'all eternity.' These are words which truly make the mind spin. Who can truly think of a world or a universe without end – no beginning, no finish? It is beyond the comprehension of man, because man's brain is limited to that in which he is living which is his body. Man's mind, linked with the consciousness that is spirit, can go way beyond the intelligence which the brain manifests, but it is often limited within itself through this great desire for proof. Once released from needing proof, accepting truth as reality, then the mind is infinite, then it can penetrate all the spheres of light within existence and can come back into the consciousness that is your individual self, having reached out and realised that time has always been in existence. There never has been a moment where time was not. So where did God come into this equation? If the soul and time are unanimous together, as always having been within the greater universes, then what gave birth to God?

The infinite mind of man
God, being the infinite mind of man, has a time of coming into existence when there was a moment within that existence that needed to project something that is finite, something that could give birth to all other things, but to do so without judgment, without the absolute need to do this, purely and simply with the recognition that God is. The I AM within all existence is God, the infinite mind; the I AM within yourself is the link with God and the I AM within the soul is the soul's infinity of existence, going back beyond the creation of the universe, back beyond the creation of the solar system. So we establish the existence of soul. We imagine in our quiet times this energy, this force, expanding and growing. Science has the perfect answer

to it – a cell, endlessly expanding itself, doubling its existence until eventually it forms into whatever the need of that initial cell may be.

Now we do not intend to give you a lesson in science; we are trying simply to create a format of understanding as to what the soul is, what it does, what it is capable of and if there is any limitation that also will be explained. Having established that the soul was purely and simply a vibratory energy, we then have to establish how it came to be a very important part of individual man. Now this is simpler, we simply take the scientific fact of the 'big bang.' What a lovely thought! The festival of light has been taking place throughout the world in many different areas over the last few weeks and there are the other light festivals which join with it progressively, even that of the old habit of burning a Guy upon a bonfire. They all create light and it is of course at a time of the year when there is a greater degree of darkness within the world than during the warmer summer months. So light plays a very great part in our understanding of the soul. Without light, which was indeed manifest by the God force, there would be no understanding of living, because light is a form of life.

Things grow in light; they do not usually grow in darkness. So as we go progressively in our minds throughout the years of history to that time when the 'big bang' exploded and became the light particles which mixed with all other particles in existence at that time, it was then that the soul 'fragmented,' as we refer to it and was able to be accepted as living forces of energy, independent from that one greater energy force which originally was Soul; but of course an energy force finds it very difficult to live apart from itself unless it can be stabilised, unless it can become a powerful energy which can be used through the mind, that linking with God, in order to create within itself. The whole of life is a business of bringing forth life, then creating death. From that death new life is created, and so on. So it was at that time that God truly came into His own magnificence. Wonderful was the thought within Him: 'Now is the time to create that which can have intelligence, which doesn't just move as one massive force, but can create its own substance, create its own being, over and over again, allowing the advancement within the universe.'

At the moment we won't think about the planetary life. Later on within this series we will, because the planetary life has its own intelligence, its own ability to create within itself individual force. In fact it is not unlike the Earth, but the Earth is so important within the universe that it had to have a very special ability to recreate within its individual soul state. So at the time of this 'big bang,' at the time when light began to exist, so everything else came into existence. It took a few million years for it to advance, to grow from a tiny microbe into a human being, but it did that and it was very important that it was allowed to do that, because without the expression of the individual soul there could be no advancement, there could be no positive link with God and with mind. Remember, God is mind, God is spirit. Spirit and mind are virtually indivisible. There is nothing yet come into existence divorced of mind. Even the minutest creature upon the Earth has the ability to think for itself, even if we call it 'instinct.' All the other parts of the body link with this. There is intelligence within just one cell of your body, let alone the greater organs which have manifested through that intelligence, through the cell which knows which part of the body it is to fashion, it is to become.

A direct link with God

So we have established that man is, or has, a direct link with the God force, a direct link with the total soul energy which goes beyond the God force. It has the ability to divide and sub-divide until it becomes a living, vibrating creature; but what makes it animate into consciousness? It is spirit and it is the spirit which gives true intelligence to everything that is around you. It encourages a flower to seed, to push its way through the earth, gradually, slowly to come from an embryo of a plant into a beautiful, scented, coloured plant in which you can delight. It allows a seed to grow into a tree that also has its own intelligence, its own spirit force. If it did not, it would not reproduce itself so faithfully throughout all its seasons – the season of rest, the season of growing forth into new life, the season of harvesting – it is all part of a rhythm and again we go back to the very beginning to find our rhythm.

To sum up this first of our talks to you, we will describe the whole of creation as a circle, a circle which has no beginning and no end, which constantly flows; and deep within that circle is the emerging of the spiral. It is of the spiral that we will speak on our next occasion. It is perhaps the most important element of growth linked with the soul that can be explained to mankind. It contains absolutely everything that is needed for the composition of man and for those things that support him within his life. During our talks with you, we will talk of man's link to his own planet, those energies within him that match absolutely the energies of the Earth upon which he treads, of the crystals within man that link with the energies of the crystals within his Earth – a little different from the crystalline structure, but not absolutely – but we will make this clear as time passes. We will probably culminate in speaking with you upon that which is so important in the link with other aspects in the universe – the stars, the planets, the sun, the moon – all of these things which, without being aware of man's existence would have no point in being there, because their energies, their motion are drawn from man, not man from them.

We hope that you have found our first little chat enjoyable and if you wish to ask us questions, maybe tell us some things that you are not very clear about, but those subjects of the future talks, don't speak of them now, because what we want to create within this book is smoothness, imagining that the great majority of the readers are coming in with an open mind, completely unaware of our approach to spiritual matter and spiritual energy. So therefore if, my children, you can speak with us on extensions of that, or more detail of that which we have opened before you on this occasion, it will give us great pleasure to answer you.

Q: I always thought that the God force created everything else, but actually if I understood correctly, you said that the soul created the God force, the creative energy within that, and this quite shocked me, because I really don't understand it so well and the second question was.....

M: Shall we take that one first? What might be a good idea is if those of you who wish to question us stand up when you give your question, then we can look into your aura, into your soul. We can see there the amount of perception that you truly have and also it might help the microphone situation.

Let us take that part of your question first. It is very easily answered. All things within Universal Law, which we have not yet touched upon, are of equal merit. What comes first, what comes later, what develops from that is truly immaterial. It is all essential within the flow of life. Without all those parts there can be no whole, so if you take our very last situation and think of that, if you think of the circle which is a flowing light, a flowing energy, never ceasing, always turning, taking everything in, blending it and moving on, moving back, moving forward, it is all part of that greater whole; and also, although for simplicity we have given you the picture of soul initially, then God, do remember within our basic philosophy of teaching everything happens in one moment. It is spread out for your infinity, for your adjustment within your life, your progress, your ability to sleep, to wake, to move, to rest, but it is actually one smooth motion. So the beginning of existence, the development of God, the development of the universe, of the planets, of the Earth itself and of everything that appeared very slowly, over a great number of years, to evolve from this, within the time aspect was immediate.

So forget, my child, about being confused; that which you have learned, that which you have studied, is perfectly correct. It is simply that we are making a little more of a meal of it! And the second part of your question?

Reply: The second question was regarding when a soul was coming into life. You said in previous teachings that within the womb of the woman during conception and later on the soul would visit the womb and go back to spirit and that actually the life force would incarnate when the child was born. So do we find that soul and spirit and the life force are united through life in that human being and what happens in death when the souls leave the body, what about the spirit, do they stay together?

M: The spirit returns to the God force from which it first emanated, but we will come to that, we think, later on. As we progress into giving you an understanding of the animation, we will actually talk of being conceived, being allowed to develop in the womb, coming into life and then returning on that circle, on that spiral, back into spirit. We will cover all of this, we promise. It is a little out of step with today's talk.

Q: Master, I think you have answered my question, but just to be entirely clear, you referred to the birth of God and to the 'big bang,' at which time the physical universe and the soul were created. Are you saying that there was no gap between the two, that everything was simultaneous?

M: Absolutely. There are some concepts which are difficult for man to accept, not to understand. It is in the conception of the idea of the oneness of everything that can sometimes confuse, but yes, you are correct in your assumption.*

Q: Master, you spoke of the spirit animating the soul. Before the spirit enters the soul, does the soul have a different type of energy?

M: It has an energy which conforms to a whole mass, without any individual particles within that mass vibrating differently or being aware of, shall we say, controversy within itself. There is nothing within that mass that could argue with another part of the mass. It is rather as if you have a little bowl which you place full of water. Now if you assume that the water is absolutely, one hundred per cent pure and do not raise the argument of the microbes etc, but within that bowl, that receptacle, there is only a mass of water, if you add something into it, whatever it may be, then you add an argument to the main mass (we are putting this in very colloquial terms). So what occurred when that mass of soul was intended to become more variant, to introduce conflict, to be part of itself but separate from itself? There had to be an action taking place which would create that. I suppose you could almost refer to it as the action of the atom, but in order to keep this at a level where people can understand the concept rather than the actual happening, we put it in that way. Do you think that is a possible way to imagine it?

Reply: Yes, I would think so. Can you say then whether this soul, or this mass, had knowing and if so, was it actually aware that it had knowing?

M: It had knowing, but it was not aware it had it.

Reply: So the introduction of conflict enabled it to be aware that it had knowledge?

*The confusion here arises from the fact that the physical universe was created by the thought aspect of God whereas the fragmentation of soul which gave rise to individualised life forms was created by the feeling or heart aspect of God. In effect there were two 'big bangs'. It is also useful to bear in mind that there is no time in the spirit realms, only an ever-present 'now' in which all things are happening simultaneously. Only in human perception are events seen to have a linear, causative progression. For further clarification see page 20. The Master explains these principles in more detail in the 'Way of Truth'.

M: It enabled it to be aware that it could gain knowledge. Although only a slight correction, it is a rather important one.

Q: From what you've been saying, I have this picture that soul was almost a homogenous energy and that the 'big bang' was rather like the coming into existence of the first cell. That what is actually happening is that we have almost a cellular growth and division of the universal soul into individual souls, in order for the growth and expansion of knowledge to take place. Would that be a correct picture of what you've been saying?

M: It would, because as you know we have discussed this together, have we not, and this has been our conclusion. So it is good that you raise it in this environment, so that those little 'touches,' shall we say, of what we have discussed, which will go into a book which is more suitable for this form of teaching, can also move into this particular book on the development of the soul in a nice, smooth, understandable way.

Q: Could I also ask a second question here? Part of my puzzlement with this whole process is what is the purpose of this activity that the universal soul is engaging in? Is it to actually expand itself by this sort of cellular growth? Is that the means by which soul reproduces itself in a sort of universal way, that we all come back to source and add to that totality?

M: That is so. It is also part of the desire within all living things for the reproduction and then the slowing down as that particular energy created for the reproduction begins to wane, as all those cells begin to live out their existence, begin to flow less actively, begin to desire within themselves to be released, no longer to reproduce, to have such activity, which of course eventually leads to the death, not only of the human body, but of nature, the animals, the plants, the trees and so forth. Everything manifesting in the earthly world, the world of matter, must eventually cease to be, it must eventually die. It is only in the spheres of light which are separate from the world – from the Earth which has this power of death and regeneration – that this principle does not exist. As you also state, when that process has reached its conclusion, when the death, we will say, of the body has manifested and the soul is released, the spirit is released, it then starts its approach to living – to birth and rebirth – all over again. Eventually, at the end of the cycle when all aspects of that soul are again retained as one mass within the soul itself, the Higher Self as we refer to it, then that Higher Self goes forward, becoming part of the God force, the living energy that supplies intelligence, pure life, pure light. It is allowed then to increase the flow of these living energies which otherwise, of course, would begin to burn out like everything burns out if it is not regenerated. So the soul energy never dies to the extent that it is unable to regenerate and to allow further manifestation of life within the planet.

Q: Master, when all the fragments go back to join the God force and become one again, will there be a further explosion and has this already occurred? In other words, have there already been other worlds and other beginnings of time and it's a continuation of the cycle, as you said, with matter becoming refined until it flows back to the other side and then condensing until it becomes physical matter again?

M: The short answer to that is yes, definitely. We might be able to enlarge on it at some time as part of the content of a longer talk, but you are correct in your summing up, in your analysis. It has already occurred several times.

Q: So is it the same souls that are coming back in different fragmentary configurations?

M: No. We say no, but that isn't strictly true. Some do, but mostly at the end of each generation of life (let us put it that way), the souls have returned, they have become part of the greater God force which can then release new energy, new life, so that the cycle begins all over again; but of course, we all know about the Children of Light and we know that they were recalled from their movement through the spiritual planes, the spheres of light, in order to be reborn, but this is virtually the only incidence and this was particularly requested by the Masters of Light in whose control existence lies.

Reply: But they were part of this existence, this cycle. (**M:** No, Atlantis completed the last cycle.) *When I refer to a cycle I mean a physical universe being created in a 'big bang.' They were part of this universe, but there have been other worlds, other universes?*

M: Now that is a little different. We would need to go into that more deeply. The actual world itself is the same, but we thought you were speaking of cycles of existence within this world. We apologise, my child.

Chairman: Perhaps if I could try and help, my understanding is that the 'big bang' you are talking about is an analogy for the explosion of consciousness that comes from the individuation of the mass of soul, due to an act of God. It is different to the 'big bang' which is the current scientific theory about the birth of the universe.

M: That is so.

Reply: But I thought from my previous question that the two were in fact simultaneous?

M: They are linked, intrinsically linked, of course they are. We do not know how to simplify this really.

Chairman: In the context that you are using it, is the 'big bang' an explosion of consciousness, described in the Genesis creation story as the fall from grace?

M: That is so.

Q: Master, when the souls return to the God force, and once again the God force becomes whole, what does it then know that it didn't know before?

M: That is a very good question. Obviously, it is not the every-day life of getting up and going to work and so forth. That is of no interest to the Higher Self at all. It is what has been achieved through spiritual awareness, through the growth of the spirit within, through the link with the God force which gives a form of intelligence which we shouldn't confuse with being able to read and write and add up. It is nothing to do with the actual brain. There have been well-known cases of people who are completely unable to have any individual expression, or who are in a vegetable state and yet they have a wonderful affinity with the spirit of God, they live in their own world of colour and light. They manifest within themselves that which otherwise can only be achieved when in the etheric body within the spheres of light. But in life (if you can call it living for them) their time is creative, it is able to commune with the Higher Self, with all aspects within it, and it learns from what is taking place externally to its body – what it needs to learn from what is taking place upon the Earth itself. For those who are more fortunate, those who can choose their pathway, choose how much they learn spiritually and how they interlink it with the material world in which they live, and with their personality which forms a very important part of their living, in this way of integration people then learn a spiritual conception within life that might not have been there before their existence. They actually contribute to others around them an essence of aware-ness, an essence of that total knowledge which they bring down through the Higher Self, through their own bodies, speaking what they feel, speaking what they see and it is on this level that the soul begins to develop, begins to gain its spiritual con-sciousness and grow and expand and become greater.

So it is not so much reading the written word, being told that this is correct and that is correct and you should under-stand this through practice. It is the way you interpret the feel-ings within yourself, whether you agree with the statement made, which after all is somebody else's conception of reality, whether your own matches up to it or extends beyond it. It is this which is reflected within your Higher Self and which is shared with all those aspects. If they have learned, however little, however great, it is then expanded into the consciousness of living, because those very small changes can make such a dif-ference to the way that others live. Wars would then cease, bit-terness, anger, conflict amongst man would not be able to exist because there would be no grounds upon which they could feed and grow. It is this that the soul learns from and shares, not only within itself, but with other souls that merge with it and learn in a similar direction.

Q: A lot of the mystics of the past spoke about 'from the one you need to create a second one' for the second to confront and juxta-pose, in order to create the third, the fourth, the fifth and sixth. Is this the exemplification of creation? How can from one be created a second just through separation? Is it through separation that there is a second force that can then be a creative force to produce the second, third, fourth, etc?

M: It has to be progressive with the sub-division of the one, in whatever way it is done. Modern science now of course allows a cell to sub-divide and become a human being without the natural process of coming together and creating life. The original concept of life has always been that of the one dividing and sub-dividing into its many parts in order to create more and more. The first human being multiplying into the millions that now live within the world was in actual fact not just a Biblical story, although not quite in the same way as the Bible expounds upon it, of course not. It goes back several million years, this initial division and sub-division. The mystics, although they are often a bit limited in the way they express themselves in the way they teach, they have the right idea, my child.

It has given us so much pleasure speaking with all of you, entering into your energy fields, being aware even amongst those who have not spoken this time of your interest and also of your soul growth, which of course we see reflected around you in your soul bodies, your auras, which are there very plain for us to see.

Until we meet on the next occasion, Shabbath Shalom!

Chapter 2

Talk Two, December

Circles and spirals. God consciousness. The relationship of thought and creation. The AUM and the birth of spirit. The I AM within the self. All things from one living source.

Master: Greetings. Shalom! As in the past we will stand and address you, as after all it is only polite, is it not, to stand at that moment of giving direction and teaching and when we have spoken sufficiently unto the time and the necessity of the moment, we will then be seated so that as you ask your questions – and we do hope that each one of you has come prepared on this occasion to speak with us – we will ask that you stand, in order that we see your aura and are aware of your presence.

Last time we were together, the subject was of the beginning of the creation of soul. Many things arose from that particular discussion which interested us a great deal and have given food for thought as to how to quench the curiosity and desire for knowledge that are obviously there within each one of you. As we said on that occasion, the main topic of discussion this day is of the circle, the spiral within it, this of course includes the God consciousness and how it relates to man and also any of those questions which will arise and others that we can speak upon. In that way each of these occasions will ultimately cover the whole subject of soul.

No beginning, no end

The circle of which we spoke is in a way a circle within a circle. All things that have no beginning and no ending are obviously a circle by their very nature. Man's comprehension of 'no beginning and no end' cannot really adjust to the magnitude of this reality. The consciousness of man always states explicitly that all things have a beginning. They must emerge from something, whether it is a seed, a root, or even a thought when it comes to discussion and learning; so this is one of those facts that those persons here and all who may read the ultimate text of the book will have to take for granted. It is not provable, how can it be? The fact remains that there has always been an existence, a universal existence, and therefore there has always been that which is within the universe that eventually gave rise to the creation and to all things which dwell within it. This of course is where science falls short, where those that are of a scientific nature find it so difficult to comprehend. Everything in their estimation must be proven, but where the spiritual is concerned very little can be truly proven. Mostly it has to be accepted because it is there, it is experienced by all men, therefore it is within experience that all things come to life, all things dwell within a consciousness of understanding, within that spiritual content of which we endeavour to share our philosophy and our knowledge with you on so many occasions.

Having established this circle from which the soul received its vital energy and which allowed the nature of God, or the Absolute which we favour as a term, to come into a contiuous existence – indeed universe without end and world without end – this God consciousness starts as a spiral of energy. Again, spirals have no beginning and no end, they are in perpetual motion, sometimes moving a little more slowly than others, sometimes within that spiral there are so many events which cover millions and millions of years, millions and millions of light years, and millions and millions of miles of space that start within that spiral and move constantly beyond it. We liken much of this to a child's humming top. When it is stationary it is so simple, a simple piece of tin usually, which with a flick of the wrist begins its movement and as that movement accelerates you become less and less conscious of the movement. It is like this with the spirals of energy which are constantly developing, moving and accelerating.

Imagine if you can the initial circle of activity, the spiral moving within it, giving rise as it spreads into infinity to many, many of these circles and spirals. Light is built up of this. If you analyse light with all its particles, with its very varied substance that is the composite of light as you are aware of it, you will see all these little spirals moving at great speed. In each particle there are millions, and yet surrounding each one is a clear circle of brilliance that merges into the light particle, giving it substance, issuing from it that which allows all things life. Without light there can be no existence of any form that breathes and moves. Without light nothing can grow; therefore in the darkness of infinite space all was still. It needed something within that silence and darkness to give birth to light. From this intense stillness that which is the Absolute gave birth to a thought. The thought was as one with sound.

When you go through a thinking process, you think that

all is quiet, there is no awareness of a sound or even a vibration around you as you sit quietly and think; but there emanates from you a sound so faint, so infinitesimal that even you are not aware of it. This is of course the difference between those that dwell in the spirit spheres and relate to the energy that is purely of spirit and that which has its roots in matter. In spirit the slightest thought gives rise to a response and it is that energy evoked by the thought that brings about a response from other spiritual beings. This is why we react so very quickly to your thought, to your desire for help, for example. There are those aspects within your Higher Self who are immediately available to give tangible help to you. You have only to link with them and you need never be afraid or alone. The only criterion that spirit asks for is trust. Once it is given, within that trust all things are possible.

Creation and thought

But to return to that thought, as light as a whisper, which flowed across the intensity of darkness – as it flowed, so it made this delicate, gentle hum. So often we refer to the sound of the universe, for once that sound was evoked it could never depart and this is so in every aspect, both within the universe and all the planetary areas and also upon the Earth where nothing is revoked once it begins. It goes on, magnified until it reaches its ultimate climax, its ultimate conclusion. When that happens, as it is caught up in the spiral all it can do is return to its lowest point and begin once more to evolve.

We call the sound of the universe the AUM. It really does have to be very, very silent wherever you are to hear it, and very few people in the modern day and age would be able to tell you what it sounds like. At the beginning of time, if you had been there then you would have known exactly what that sound relates to. That sound, that movement within the universe, was the birth of spirit. Spirit moves within light and allows light to magnify and grow, like the sunrise sweeping across the horizon after a dark night.

From the light, from the beginning of spirit, you then have the creation of a living soul. We don't propose to reiterate all that we said on the last occasion, you can link that together with our preamble at this moment, but we were quite anxious that you would have a complete knowledge of what the God consciousness was comprised of, to be aware that that sound, that energy, that light, that spirit, is in its total God, expressed in thought, expressed in the movement of the circle and the spirals, filling the whole of infinity so that there is no area anywhere that does not contain that spirit which is God. Now how does it relate to what is taking place within man?

Man has a consciousness which has been evoked by that spirit entering the soul at the time of birth, but how can the consciousness within man allow that God consciousness to be experienced? It is experienced through awareness of self initially, then the awareness of everything that encircles the self which comes a little later, after the birth of a child, because the child is only aware initially of self and then of those that attend to its needs. Gradually there is the understanding that there are others that move into its environment. It experiences cold, warmth, uncomfortableness and bliss – all those areas that allow the inner consciousness to blend with that of the God consciousness, the Absolute. This remains throughout conscious life and this includes any period of unconsciousness, whether it is sleep or whether it is anaesthetised, or because of a coma. Any form of quiet, rest, oblivion, doesn't count; the two consciousnesses blend as one.

There *is* a God
So those who say and genuinely believe it, 'there is no God' don't know what they are talking about, and one of your little tasks as a result of the knowledge that you imbibe is to be able to say to those people how wrong they are. You can only do this if you have some facts at your disposal, facts which they can accept for one of two reasons – they cannot disprove you or they cannot to their own satisfaction disprove what is being said in this particular spiritual way. It is so simple to say to another, 'But you have a consciousness which blends within the universe, within the creation of that universe. You cannot be separated from it because you emerged from it and you return into it.' There are many steps along the way, but everyone, everything has to have a beginning. Whether you look at an individual cell and see within it life beginning to be created, or whether you see that which is shrivelled, which has completed its cycle of existence, but has awareness that it still continues through that veil of spirit where the consciousness moves to a different vibration, a much faster vibration of understanding that is beyond man's capability, there is only one particular form

of consciousness. It relates to the soul, it relates also to mind which has also grown from within that spiral of activity that has itself arisen from that first sound emitted by that first breath.

The Holy Book that is read by millions, understood even by those that follow different faiths, refers to the breath of God moving into the stillness from which life emerged, but to imagine it, to have a blueprint of it, is so very different. We spoke last time of the vastness of soul and one of the questions we remember was whether or not there was a conscious awareness within that mass, and our answer to this was 'not within the mass, but within the particles of that mass there was the ability to gain knowledge.' But how can anything, whatever it may be, gain knowledge without some understanding of what knowledge is being gained, whether it is important, whether it is outside the acceptance of reality, or whether it is a substance that is worthy of duplication or of acceptance? It is because it again relates constantly back within that spiral, moving so fast you cannot see it, drawing from the beginning that which is there within its consciousness to be learned from. When it is within the body, when it is the soul which, remember, exists in its particles in every cell within the body, when it is trapped, as it were, within an individual, it must then have the next and virtually the last important ingredient added to it, which is the free will. It is this that sets man apart from animals and certainly from any other creation that is worthy of discussion. Man, because of his ability to make his own decisions, to share his thoughts, has a very special task and that task is to relate to his Earth, to take care of his Earth and to take care of the rest of humanity. That you can call the love principle. Again, the love principle is God.

The I AM within the self
So you have a package within the God consciousness which contains all the ingredients that humankind needs in order to live a harmonious life, a life where everything is possible as long as it is understood that no harm is done to another and no limitations are placed upon the ability of the self, whether it is to conquer fear, to conquer violence, or excesses of any kind. A complete awareness within the self of what God is requiring from humanity that was fashioned after His own self, His own heart, His own soul, His own being. We have a term that describes it all – the I AM within the self. The I AM is that God

consciousness reverberating throughout all existence and being drawn into the individual as each particle represents the whole.

We have not covered a great deal of ground in this talk because we felt that to understand the important principle of life – that light, love, soul, thought, movement, ability, free will, all these things emanate from the one living source – is the most important teaching which will arise again and again as we go through the material of this book. If this is not understood, if this is not accepted, thrashed out as it were, at this time, it is pointless to continue. When we have spoken throughout the years, although we expected it, it has been a disappointment when those that have been so long in reading the teachings that emanate from us do not seem to understand the First Principle, which is God – still looking at the personal God, still looking at the existence of creation as something that happened within the lifetime of man – so we felt among ourselves that as long as this principle is accepted, understood and experienced, we can then go forward with the remaining times with you and share a great deal of knowledge which will benefit all.

So now we look forward to your questions and we never mind how many times we go over the same ground, as long as it is understood.

Q: Master, I don't quite undertand how when we first experience the uncomfortableness when we are born, how this is a clue to binding our energy with the God consciousness. Could you expand on that please?

M: In actual point of fact the child does not experience discomfort at the moment of birth, because the ability to feel discomfort or pain has not been awakened within the cells of the brain. This is the main reason why it is not possible for the infant to remember the birth, whether it is at the time or when the adult goes through either an inner awareness of thinking about birth and what may possibly have caused different problems within the life, being aware as they think of that passage from the mother into the world. They cannot. They can only remember what has been said to them at different times within life, whether it is as a young child or when much older, when the mother expresses the difficulty of the birth, or the anxieties or the fears. It is then and then only that a person remembers on a certain level, but not on an actual level. The cortex of the brain is such that creation has specifically ensured that the birth process is painless for the child. So whether it is a Caesarean, a forceps delivery, a breech birth or a natural birth, the child is only aware from that moment when the first cry is uttered and even then there is no sense of pain or discomfort. This comes about in varying degrees, from a matter of days to some weeks. In fact some physicians feel that a child can even be operated upon without any form of anaesthetic until it is a month or six weeks old, but because it varies with each child as to when the cells within the brain develop the ability to feel pain, we would not advocate this. But you asked, did you not, how it affects a person later on in life, was that your meaning?

Reply: No Master, I believe you said that when the child begins to have knowledge that there are others within its realm of consciousness, it then began – I think the word you used was 'an uncomfortableness' – and it was only at this time that it was aware of its bond with the God consciousness. I don't think 'bond' was the word you used, but you were indicating that it was then aware.

M: Yes, it is a dawning of the awareness of what is taking place around, which is all part of the expanding process of the consciousness within, the ability to know whether there is love being extended toward it, or anxiety, or even dislike, because a very young child works on a similar vibration to that of a young animal. It senses motivation within others, it senses that it is being offered refreshment or being offered comfort. We were thinking rather more of placing the child in the comfort of arms, rather more than comfort in a bodily sense, but this of course is just as important, because as these cells within the brain begin to multiply and to create a sense of pain, so the child is then aware from an outer source of what is taking place within its little world.

Q: You mentioned that there was a stillness and darkness and the birth of God. Was the Absolute alone before the thought came and did the thought come out of aloneness? Was the Absolute there in that stillness and then the thought came?

M: Yes indeed, the Absolute, the God force, the energy which is God, was you might say without any movement of life. It was there, but absolutely still. The consciousness within it had yet to be awakened. It is rather like when you are waiting for that first chord of music which begins a much-awaited concert. You see all the players with their instruments, sitting so quietly, bows raised, for that wave of the baton, that encompassing movement of the conductor. It is breathless. Suddenly the conductor raises his arms and the first chord of the symphony overcomes, gently, quietly, almost soundlessly, or with a great crash of cymbals and all instruments beginning. If you can hold on to that thought of holding the breath, that waiting for that first sound, that describes how the energy of God, how this Absolute Understanding waited with such quietness for the right moment when everything within the universe had reached exactly that point of stillness within the darkness. You could almost imagine It holding Its breath and then emitting it at that exact moment of opportunity. The consciousness was there, it simply was not vibrating. It was in this quiet stillness that the motivation had to take place for the action to follow. So the brain was there, you might say, although more accurately we would say the mind was there and that mind was already linking with everything that would be achieved from that breath, from that thought. Is this what you were meaning?

Reply: Yes, so it was like a vision before the thought.

M: You could very accurately put it that way – waiting motionless for that moment to occur.

Q: My question is along the same lines. I got hung up on the idea of sound creating light because it seems that is what you implied, or is sound sort of a by-product? We are told that God said in the beginning, 'Let there be light,' but was it actually a first thought, or sound?

M: Even the light had to emerge from something. All these analogies, all these words as they are expressed, whether it is in a book that was as thoughtful and well-expressed as the Holy Book, whether it is within the Torah, whether it is within any of the books and laws which relate to people within the world, always there is something missing because however clever the scholar, they cannot always get every full stop and comma right. So we stick with what we said, my child, in that particular order.

Reply: I wasn't so bothered about whether it was spoken or thought, it was more that I somehow thought that light came before sound and the speed of light is so much faster than the speed of sound.

M: It was definitely sound, which was the breath exuding across the stillness of the universe. Faint it might have been, but you try emitting your breath without making a sound. It is in fact said in the book that God breathed across the firmament and then said, 'Let there be light.'

Q: My question is in relation to birth and when soul and spirit become united in matter. I would like to know if when the body dies soul and spirit remain united throughout eternity.

M: Initially the spirit, which has given the animation of life in the first place, moves away from the body, allowing it to enter into the different phases of death. It is very closely followed by soul. It is almost a simultaneous movement, but we would say that spirit has the edge on the movement. Again, it is emitted through the breath. As people pass from one life into another this spirit is exuded, the breath is emitted from the body. As this takes place, generally through the oral cavity of the mouth, so the soul will follow. It can be through the crown chakra, it can be through the solar plexus, but they are then individual. The spirit belongs to the God force, the God consciousness; the soul, because it has been a particle within humanity for however many years that person has lived, has now an individuality which cannot lose its sense of understanding. Whatever it has learned throughout the course of the life remains within it. Even when it is joined once more with any Higher Self and all other aspects it still keeps that individual awareness of progress within itself. It shares with all others, it shares with those aspects that have not lived or had the opportunity of life and it shares with those that have already absorbed the experience of life and are no longer able to come back into existence. It is important that they share all that has taken place within the whole, to keep a balance, to keep an awareness as time goes fleeting on and maybe a personality needs that help, needs that comfort from one of the aspects as it is finding its way through life. So everything must be shared within the whole and the balance that takes place because of this action also allows the main need of the Higher Self to fulfil itself. We spoke briefly on this in the previous talk and we will of course speak again, because all of these things are so relevant and to repeat them is often necessary to link one part of our teaching with another.

That is the way the soul and spirit exit from the body, which immediately becomes lifeless. All the vital signs cease, the heart stops, there is no movement within the brain. The mind, which is you might say 'on loan' to the body during life, also returns to its greater capacity of knowledge. We have in the past, because people found it difficult with the concept of mind, referred to it as a 'deep and silent pool' into which everything merges and from which everything exudes and it is a good simile because the mind itself is never chaotic. It is the way that humanity treats its thoughts and those things that emerge from the thoughts that appear to make thought and mind a chaotic principle, but it is not – it is indeed the quietest aspect within humanity. Those who refer to the 'unquiet mind' could not be more wrong. The mind is evoked within meditation and meditation truly cannot be chaotic if it is approached in the correct manner.

Q: Are humankind the first beings in creation that have embodied an individualised soul?

M: Yes.

Reply: Why?

M: That is an excellent question, my son and very worthy of you! Because the God principle wanted something to express Itself, Its own knowledge, in a tangible way. Although the rest of creation was so beautiful and expressed the beauty within itself, there was no animation, there was no ability to converse, to share. The mind does not exist in the same way in the other aspects of creation as it does in humankind, so it was with a very special need within Itself that the Absolute created man, knowing that with all the different composite parts it would evolve and grow. The expression of the knowledge contained within the Absolute would also be contained within this creature who would expand and grow throughout the centuries, throughout the ages, achieving ultimately precisely the same knowledge as the Absolute, at which time humanity will merge with the Absolute with all its spiritual force and man will no longer be a necessary commodity upon the Earth. It is doubt-ful whether the Earth itself, since it was created for man, would even be necessary within the universe, as indeed all the other planetary life is very necessary to keep the Earth within its orbit.

Q: Master, it occurred to me that all the principles you have described about the creation and about the soul are literally recre-ated within our own processes every day, like giving birth to a thought. It's the same thing, it precedes the tension, the motivation, the thought, the action and so on. So in a sense the more we look at it, we are actually a living example of the very principle that you have just described and as part of that whole picture I wanted to ask you, having mentioned earlier the principle of love and that nothing can exist without light, how does the light of the Christos bring its influence to bear on our consciousness and how does it guide the pathway of the soul?

M: The Christos is spiritual love. It is love of a far faster and greater capacity than the love principle which exists in man. The First Principle, the Creator, the Absolute, while being exactly the same, cannot have form – it is totally formless. The creation within man to give rise to the ability that is within the First Principle must contain all the same ingredients, as you would say, in order that the mind has the ability to put into action what the thought creates. If the Absolute had been able to create within Itself a body, all of the living creation expressed upon the Earth would not have been necessary. Once man had reached a certain optimum understanding and linking with the Absolute, the next stage was available to issue forth and that was the creation of the Christos in form. It had existed in its formless capacity, enabling the spiritual love principle to develop and grow throughout the initial stages of mankind's development. When man truly reached that time of the ability to understand and differentiate between the spiritual and the world of matter, the world of action, of living, of developing within itself, then of course God was able to allow a living entity, Yeshua, to be born upon the Earth, embodying that Christos, that selfless love, that totality of blending with the Absolute, but also to understand because of action, because of going through the birth process in the same way as all other beings, to understand and link the Christos with humanity. This is why it would not be possible for a similar event ever to take place again. Once this has been shown within an aspect of humanity it is achieved, it is there.

It is the same with anything on Earth – once it is created you can change the pattern but the blueprint remains the same. Everything else emerges from it. A cottage can become a mansion or a palace, but it has emerged from the thought and the action in building the cottage. So when the Christos came into man in the form of Jesus, of Yeshua, that act of creation was established.

When there is talk of the second coming, when there was the linking of the Children of Light and a possible leader of the Children of Light being linked with the second coming, we all shivered. It is man's inability to understand even the life force principle of one thing being created and giving rise to another in a slightly different form, being unable to accept this, which is always such a problem for spiritual teachers. There will be acknowledged leaders of the Children of Light. There may even be one that will embody within him or herself all the light manifestation that is needed to allow those children to fulfil their individual purposes. When this occurs there will be a bringing together of those children in the same way as a general will lead his soldiers into battle, but it will be a spiritual battle, it will be a battle of good over evil, of light over darkness; but there cannot be a second coming of a principle which is part of the First Principle – an extension of that life force which God, the Absolute, is.

Many times we attempt to explain the difference between Yeshua the man and the Christos – Yeshua the Christ. Generally speaking Yeshua the Christ emerged from Yeshua the man at the time of His passing from the earthly body into the etheric. When people speak of Jesus the Christ it is of His mission within the Earth in His etheric self, His proving of the triumph of life over death, the ability to be able to express His Soul's purpose within that etheric self, triumphant from the understanding man had had up to that time, that once his body died there was nothing left of him to survive. That was His task. The fact that it has been wrongly interpreted, misrepresented, was because of the great difficulty in writing at that time in such a way that all of humanity could understand. The passing by word of mouth was also inconsistent because of language. But at this time, as the age of Aquarius emerges from the morass of ignorance of the past, when mankind has the ability at last to accept that there are those in spiritual realms who can speak through others, there is a wonderful chance of the truth being expressed, accepted and shared. This is of course one of the most important aspects of our work – that of Father Abraham, of Elijah and of myself – to get this knowledge across to the greatest number of people that can both understand and accept, as these are two very different principles within life. So the Christos can be termed the love principle contained within the First Principle of existence.

Q: Based on the coming of Christ and man's ability to accept maybe a new pathway, man has distorted Yeshua's teaching through interpretation of language. Maybe it's a controversial thing to say but in some ways it has caused more harm to man – the distortion and the coming of Christ – than the love principle which was supposed to come through. I am just thinking that all the wars might have been averted without the coming of Yeshua.

M: We doubt it very much – there would have been another excuse for a war if they had not had the controversy which arose over whether He was Christian or Jew and what His message was. It arose of course at that time because the Jews were waiting for a leader, they were waiting for a Jehovah who would bring them freedom, bring them a way that they could express their awareness of love. They were waiting for a figure which would express itself in its manhood as a king, as a leader, as someone that would rally the troops into action. What everyone, whatever their beliefs or their origins were, found very difficult to accept was the true message that He brought. They couldn't divorce the man from the principle; they couldn't divorce His ability to express love in its true form, which is of course the infinite capacity to heal, nor in the spoken message, even though language was no problem to Him. All those that He spoke with, whether to a vast crowd or to one or two, they understood utterly His verbal remarks because language did not truly exist – they listened to vibration. They listened to the movement within themselves expressed through knowledge.

So it is a fact, a truth – everyone must have an excuse in order to provoke some action, whether it is an instinctive dislike or mistrust of another race, or whether it is greed, fear, all these many things which arise within humanity to create strife. If they did not have what they consider a fixed objective to fight over it would be something else and unfortunately that will always exist until man has become so refined, so aware within himself of that, that he realises war and strife are aimless, non-objective things to evoke.

Q: I feel a slight confusion which is to do with the individual aspect of soul which incarnates upon this Earth. There seems to be a controversy, or dichotomy when reading your words. Part of your words say that we have just the one existence and the other says that we reincarnate. My own experience is of feeling greater than just the aspect, that there is something within which is connected with all reincarnations and that there is a memory where one has appeared to have lived before or been somewhere before, or remembers. Could you say whether we do consist of something which is greater than the aspect which has incarnated? Is there something permanent within us?

M: That which is greater is the Higher Self in its totality. It is in the sharing that has taken place at the end of all other lives by the individual aspect that does of course dwell in the memory pattern of man. That memory is linked very closely with mind, and as the thoughts are part both of mind and also of brain – brain being the instrument that gives rise to the thought (you might say it is like the electrical pattern moving through a machine) – so the thought pattern does enable both the individual in his human form and the aspect that is in harmony with every cell within his body to relate to what has happened in the past.

You *are* your past, you *are* the exemplification of all actions from all aspects throughout your life. There is a particular motivation within the Higher Self for particular lessons to be exemplified and therefore, whether there are fifty aspects alive at the same time within the world or only one, that purpose is the same for all but is achieved by the individual which allows it to become active, allows it to be that machine, achieved by the individual in whatever way their circumstances will permit it – the colour of their skin, their beliefs, the part of the world in which they are born, the kind of society in which they live – all of these things are very important for the release of that purpose to take place. You are probably aware, all of you, as you read our teachings on these matters, how important it is that the whole of the continents and lands are visited in different lifetimes by the different aspects, to be aware of different beliefs, different abilities, from the very simplest and most primitive to that of the most advanced nation.

So the individual aspect has only that life, there is only one personality for it. In your case there is you, as the personality, there is the aspect living, experiencing, growing within you and when your body is no longer required and returns as they say, 'Dust to dust and ashes to ashes,' the soul lives on, the aspect lives on, but it does not return again to the Earth.

We hope, my children, that by reiterating different teachings a pattern emerges, a pattern that enables not only yourselves but those who eventually will read them to have a clearer perspective of how important it is that the best possible use is made of the life you are now in. It will not be repeated, not one moment of it will be reiterated. What you've done, what you've been, is relegated to the past within seconds of it occurring, but what does remain is motivation, learning, what you have achieved on an understanding level, what you have absorbed within you, the knowledge of how to progress, how to go forward, how to change. Have we not endlessly spoken, individually and en masse, of accepting change and moving forward? As you do that you change the whole motivation of the Earth itself with every other individual accepting, changing, moulding, being. Whether you can accept totally that first initial stage of having come into existence within the God force and emanating from that or not, you have to accept that you are now, you are who you are and the principle alive within yourself was sufficient unto this life and unto none other.

Until our next talk with you, our love remains, it never changes. It is the one constant thing that you can all depend upon. Our thanks for your understanding and your concentration. My children, farewell. Shalom.

Chapter 3

Talk Three, January

The spheres of light. Planets and planetary life. The unique relationship of man to God. The Archangels of Light. The Christos. Animals and Soul.

Master: Beloveds, shalom!

All: Shalom, Master.

M: In general we have given a great deal of thought toward the discussion on the soul, trying to make it as comprehensible as possible and yet still covering all the ground that is necessary, not only for those who are here listening and taking part, but also for those who will ultimately read the words. It has not been an easy decision as to what can be, as it were, 'skimmed over,' and what should be gone into in greater depth. Always there is in mind the fact that over the years it is a subject that has been well-discussed and taught by all of your spiritual teachers and we have tried to put this to one side when making the decision as to in what depth we should indeed go.

We have received a great deal of help from those interested in this subject, some of whom have come and have asked specific questions in their own personal trances with us, which we know will be able to be included. Very recently the whole of one of these private trances was devoted to the subject of the spheres of light, where the soul dwells after passing; therefore we do not intend to go into any great depth over that particular area. [*The discussion is reproduced at the end of this chapter*] We know that the person concerned is here present, and if he likes to give a brief resumé as to the main subject of that trance, it will help you all to understand why we are not broaching it again. Of course, if you have questions at the end of this session and we are quite prepared to stay as long as you need, then they will be welcomed by us and answered in depth. So my son, if you would like to share with others here the main subject that we spoke on.

Reply: *I asked for an explanation of the spheres of light that exist within the spirit form, exactly what happens as the soul moves through each sphere from the moment of passing up to the place* *from where the Master speaks to us at the moment. He tells us of all that the soul goes through, each of the spheres of light from the moment of passing all the way to the golden sphere and the God force itself.*

M: Thank you, my son, that has been very helpful. Now, today's subject we felt would be to incorporate other areas within existence, within the world of spirit and indeed the entire universe, when and where there is soul present. We have said from time to time that soul is not present in all aspects of the universe and this is indeed the case. The planetary system does not have soul; it has intelligence, it has intelligent life upon each of the planets. There is intelligence to a certain degree where the stars form their particular duties, but it is not soul because it is not independent in its thought patterns, in its awareness of movement – past, present and future. All that is present in the solar system as such is present due to the under-standing of the now, and what those particular planets have as their function within the whole.

The planets and their relationship to Earth
It is generally understood, we are sure, that without all the planets the Earth itself could not exist; therefore all of the planets were created before the Earth was even considered, millions of years indeed before the Earth became a possible fact, in order that God's will, God's intelligence, the love aspect, could reverberate throughout the universe from the Earth. We have been approached from time to time by people who have desired to know from which planet they had emerged. These are not people who are ignorant of the workings of soul, they are people who know well the pattern of reincarnation, but they have felt for various reasons a link with one planet or another. There are others who have read some of the books that have already been published upon that very topic. Some have been spoken to through mediumship by speakers reputed to have emanated their intelligence from the planetary realms and have been convinced of the genuineness of both medium and the entity speaking. So this has made our task rather more difficult. On some occasions when we have been quite specific in our replies to their questions we have received the retort that we either don't know what we are talking about, or we wish to keep people in ignorance regarding their background and that

perhaps in the odd case their intelligence is greater because they have come from such a source, As our teaching has not yet reached that particular boundary and as we have nothing to say about it, why don't we just own up to being ignorant?! This kind of remark is not easy to take, even for a spiritual teacher, because we know a great deal regarding those particular planetary energies. It is not through ignorance that we speak in that way, it is through knowledge, and unfortunately those people who feel that they are being approached through planetary intelligence and that those beings have much to say of advantage to man are under a misapprehension. It is quite true; that form of intelligence can approach mankind. They do have something they wish to impart, but at this stage in the development of the universe it is not truly to man's advantage.

We will remind you of the descent of man. God, from the golden sphere, decreed within His own intelligence that man should emulate His knowledge, His love and His ability to heal, to uplift and to follow a pattern of growth which is both important for man's progress and also important for his world and all the worlds which surround him. It is only man that can have knowledge of the spheres of light which surround his world; it is only man, when he passes into the spirit energy, that can inhabit those spheres referred to recently in our friend's trance. Each sphere with its own colour, its own energy, its own vibration, is very important to the ability of man to go forward, both intellectually when on the Earth and reincarnating and spiritually as he moves through the spheres toward the God force, to become part of that initial energy of the Christos, which is beyond the goldenness of God and into the clear, bright light of eternity.

The origin of the planets

So where indeed do these planets come into the importance of man's life here on Earth? It is through their own energies and the way that this extends around the planets, linking one with another, embracing the Earth within their particular lights, their particular awareness of intelligence, linking specifically with the intelligence of the Earth, not that which grows from the Earth, not that which lives upon it, but of the Earth itself keeping it in orbit, keeping it moving in the rhythm of the other planets, all of which have their own function and have had such for many billions of light years. The intelligence which is within those planets does, to a large extent, wish to extend to the Earth, to allow the Earth to increase its awareness of its own need, not to be subject to mankind with his comings and goings and his neglect. Of course to a large extent we have sympathy with them because man is the source that looks after his Earth and several times has led to its virtual collapse, departure, and of course it has been the intervention of the spiritual teachers and there are very many of these, which has prevented the Earth becoming a lightless, energyless vehicle moving in an undisciplined manner like flotsam in space. We have our own way, quite outside of communication in this manner, of linking together and enabling changes to take place in mankind's discipline so that they can no longer have free will when it comes to this colossal destruction. Sometimes we desire to see how far man will go, how much he truly understands about the stability of the rock upon which he lives. It is always sad to realise that the ego, the desire for power, will often supersede the love of the Earth itself and has harshly brought about destruction in centuries past.

Now who else other than the spiritual teachers, who are of course part of soul, can indeed help in this form of endeavour? The Archangels of Light, they do not and never have lived upon the Earth in the same way as humankind. They have come to the Earth in the early stages of its ability to grow, to become a place of habitat. We have spoken of this many times when we have spoken of early man – not only the primitive man that you learn about in history, but early mankind linked with the spirit energies of the spheres of light at the beginning of habitable time when millions upon millions of years of oceans, of winds, of penetrating rain ceased to be and the world calmed down and became a place of beauty. It was then and not before that the Archangels of Light and other beings from those spheres were able to come to the Earth and from them came the first breed of mankind, the first intelligence to be shared from God within humankind.

It is not our intention on this occasion to go in depth with all these different stages of man's development. It is not within the parameter of learning of soul, but we do wish at least those present here and any others who will subsequently read our words, to know the difference between soul and straightforward intelligence of the mind. Picture again the source, the white light of the Christos which permeates absolutely everything within the universe, giving it life. So those who were planning to say that the planets surely must have life, of course they must, but they don't get it from the God source, they get it from beyond that, from the source of the Christos. Just for a moment, relinquish your understanding of the Christos and Christ. Think instead of the very beginning and how that white light moved across the firmament, penetrating the darkness and bringing life where before none existed, so many billions of years ago that man couldn't possibly reckon when, not even with the aid of his computers. From this energy came the planetary system.

Planetary life forms

Now you might ask if it is possible to channel energy fields from some of these planets to Earth through a medium to those who wish to listen. What is it, how do they link, how do they find voice in order to be able to do this? They don't. That which communicates is that which is outside of the actual planetary area itself but wishes to be part of that energy, restored within itself, within its own compact form, as part of the planet, but not a being as you are beings. It is rather more an energy, as you would describe a microbe or something which is capable of bringing life into force, becoming something else as it develops and grows. It is infinitesimal in its ability to share, to bring love, any more than a microbe can radiate love. It purely radiates an energy from which it can grow. It is God, the God source which brings the love and as it does not radiate throughout the planetary system, love cannot grow. The microbe can grow and it can bring a great deal of energy from its source into whatever it is communicating to. This is why some of the messages that come through mediums have very little in the way of enlightenment, the sharing of peace, the sharing of love and humility, because they do not know of it, it is not integral to themselves.

Can you imagine a worm radiating love to anything at all? You can see a worm, you can feel it, you can watch it, but you can't communicate with it; but if that worm for some reason became part of something that had intelligence and was able for the point of argument to draw from that intelligence something it could communicate with and share, you could be forgiven for thinking that at least that worm was able to share intelligence with you, but it would be getting it from an intelligent source, not from itself. So those that communicate from some of the planets are riding on the shoulders, as it were, of some of the entities which have lived upon the Earth, have absorbed a certain amount of teaching and truth and therefore through that medium they are able to communicate.

We do not expect everyone present immediately to say, 'Ah, that's fine, I believe that implicitly.' Of course it needs discussion, it needs deep thought, it needs some proof. If you really look at what these entities are sharing and compare it with the love and the true teaching from the God force, deep inside yourself, within the heart chakra and within your knowledge of what is right, you will begin to accept the possibility and the impossibility of those things that we share with you. The Angels of Light, the Archangels and all those that work in conjunction with the spiritual energy – that is very, very different. Where they communicate there is an extraordinary depth of love and they will do so more and more as this age of enlightenment begins to proceed and develop. Many of the Children of Light will be aware of these angelic creatures in all their different forms, will be able to communicate in some cases with them. We would not begin to argue with them that they do not exist, and yet for centuries parents have said to their children, 'Fairies don't exist.' But fairies do, and fairies as we have said before have their very important work to do in nature Those that inter-communicate between human beings, radiating love, bringing the divine force to play in procuring health, also have an extremely important role to play. The Archangels of Light themselves communicate incessantly within their thoughts, within their minds, between the Teachers of Light and the God energy Itself.

The Soul of animals
So everything that descends from the golden plane, the golden light of the Absolute, radiates within the energy of soul, man being the lowest of the species to be able to contact this and to share it, one with another and allow it to radiate back and forth. Now the animal world surely, you say, there must be soul amongst at least some species. All right, forget about the insects, we know that they are the lowest form of life on the Earth and they move entirely by instinct, which is of course a form of intelligence, but the animals that we love so dearly, what of them? They do have soul, but they have soul according to their species. The cat family, they have a soul to which all

relate, not the individual, but as a mass, as all the cat family. There is this irradiation of soul, so all of them are rather likely to revert back to their origins if they are removed from human society, who have allowed them to develop love, to develop a one-to-oneness with those who care for them. They can soon become wild if ill-treated or neglected.

On this point there have been many questions to us over the years: 'Will my animal be where I go when I die?' the answer is a wholehearted yes! And why? Because of your closeness to the little creature, be it cat or dog, or whether it is a form of mouse, it doesn't really matter; the rapport has built up within the family group and allowed the little creature to participate with you in your day-to-day life. It has become obedient to a large extent, it accepts and understands commands. Whether or not it obeys them depends very much upon the mood that the animal might be in at that moment. Oh yes, he understands them, but his own free will might very well lead to a good ignoring of what has been said and do not human beings do this also? It is not every human being that jumps when asked to jump. So in a way it is very intelligent for an animal to decide to ignore an order that it doesn't agree with, and yes, when that animal dies it will go to a sphere of light where, when the time comes for the human being that it cares for to come into spirit, it will be there, along with many others that have pre-deceased that person and there will be rejoicing and happiness once more; and no, they will not go for each other because they are jealous. The spirit life is the spirit life, there are not the thoughts of humanity within the spirit life. There are the attributes, the forgiveness, the understanding, the love and the sympathy, they are there in spirit, not the anxieties, the angers, the bitterness, the fighting and the hatred. So one animal lives in its soul energy with total commitment to any other animal that is also attached to you in life. The animal world is indeed the last of the species to share soul. The birds of flight, they do not share soul. They have instinct, pure instinct, which helps their survival and enables them to propagate their species.

So you have the Teachers of Light, the Archangels and all their minions, humankind, the larger animals that have a brain and a mind that can be linked with. They are available to the energy of soul, which is another word for the energy of love. Everything on the perimeter, the planetary life, is not able to propagate itself, it cannot duplicate itself, but it has the ability, as indeed does the world, to regenerate itself in order that it remain in orbit, that it be part of its pure structure, but that would be a talk on chemistry and it is not our intention in these talks to step outside the limit of spiritual teaching. You can do that another time, by reading a different sort of book, but not one that is enlightening you and others who may read it on the way of soul.

Q: I'm interested to see how your perspective works with what they have been doing with genetics at the moment. They are talking about making genetically engineered human beings and various other things, making people outside of the normal way.

M: Well, of course, from a human point of view, from the flesh and bones and everything that is within a human being, they can do this, but they cannot gain soul from anywhere other than the divine force, therefore that mysterious ingredient that prevails through every cell within the body would be absent. You would have an animal or a human being that can respond to what is around it but cannot give emotion toward things. Those who may see such a creature growing into adolescence and adulthood, expressing absolutely no emotion, no caring for the rest of humanity or for animals, would not wish to be around them very much. Also of course there is this point as to how much the spirit energy from the white light could indeed remain within such a creature, as we would call them, long enough to grow up. As you know, with the basic birth pattern when the embryo comes into the world as the child, the first thing that occurs is the spirit coming into the body and animating it into life with the soul. So the spirit, the soul and the human aspect all blend together, all set for life upon the Earth as a pattern of reincarnation. Now where does reincarnation come in, for goodness sake, with something developed from a laboratory? We assume you are speaking not of those that have had the merging of cells, of the sperm and the egg together to create life. That is quite different, that is humanity; that is exactly the same as if it was created within the womb, it is simply that it is initially created in laboratory conditions; but if you are speaking of the purely energetic form of genetics, then our answer should suffice.

Q: You were saying essentially that angels were part of the soul mass, so that would imply that they are a product of the fragmentation as well?

M: The answer to that is yes.

Reply: But not all soul incarnates, so where is the line drawn, for example with the angels and Els and Masters that never incarnate on the Earth?

M: We did not say that.

Reply: Well, I understand that some do and some don't, but angels don't incarnate, for instance.

M: No, but they have millions of years ago come to the Earth and they have the possibility. You must remember that they wouldn't stand there with beautiful wings and a lovely gown if and when – and sometimes they do if things warrant it – they come to the Earth and they would look like you all do here, in a body. That's who the Els were.

Reply: You've also referred to the gods before, saying that the gods of our myths and legends weren't all mythical. Some of them existed and walked the Earth, so where do they fit into this whole process and in the hierarchy?

M: Free will. Never leave the process of free will out of your reckoning. If they want to incarnate, to come to the Earth and go through the whole pattern, then they can do so, providing there is a host willing to allow this to happen, a mother and a father initially.

Reply: But they don't need to, they don't have the same need as humanity, so what creates that need?

M: Usually earthly conditions. Perhaps a terrible disaster which could lay the Earth waste, such as atomic warfare. If that had gone ahead at the end of the last world war and a couple of times since then, then the Earth would have been laid to waste. There might have been one or two areas where man could have lingered for a while, until he either starved to death or his burns were so severe that he would die in any case – but those would be probable points of intervention.

Reply: But they come in order to help out, whereas humanity enters a reincarnational cycle for a different reason and doesn't really have the choice, that's the way we are programmed. So where is the dividing line in the hierarchy of soul?

M: Oh but there is a choice. Where the Higher Self is concerned it has so many aspects that not a fraction of them, even over hundreds and thousands of years, could possibly come to the Earth. There is a sort of levelling process within the Higher Self as to whether it is expedient to come at this time or that time or not at all, we agree to that, but no aspect is turned down flat if it feels that there is a process that it can help toward by coming into life.

Q: If you liken the parts of soul to cells in the body, then would you say that the angels and the gods were maybe heart cells?

M: Yes, we would acknowledge that.

Q: My question is about free will. At one point I thought you said that free will might be taken from humankind and it was given to see how far man would go. Is it then in the plan for free will to be taken away from man?

M: Certainly not in the forseeable future, not during the Age of Aquarius, nor yet Capricorn that follows. The whole of the question of life upon the Earth beyond that point is in question; but free will is always limited, in any case. If it does not come within the logic of the universe, then it cannot be granted.

Q: I also wasn't clear about the God force, the Christos and the white light. Is it that love comes from the golden God force and the light from the Christos is everything else? (**M:** That is so.) *Does that mean to say that the white Christos light has no love? Could you give an explanation about the difference in the love aspect?*

M: It has the ability for love, everything has that ability, but it is the origin of intelligence. If you think that intelligence can motivate love but without intelligence you can neither feel the emotion of love nor yet recognise it in anything else. You can see that what lies above the Absolute, which is the love force, can radiate within it as it comes through it, but the intelligence which allows that love to manifest came after the Christos.

Q: Are we connected?

M: Everything is connected within the entire universe. It is full of energy fields. If it was disconnected there would be a terrible heap somewhere.

Q: You spoke about the energies that come from all of the planets toward the Earth and if all the planets have intelligence, then they have an awareness of their role within the brotherhood of planets. Earth, you've said, is the youngest of the planets, so is it still learning its intelligence from the other planets?

M: No, it is not still learning, it is very much part of that intelligence, but where it is different is that it is subject to the will, the whim of that which develops upon it. The other planets do not have living, growing things which depend upon the soil beneath and the crystallisation deep within the Earth's body, emanating from the centre. So the Earth is very dependent upon what it harbours, what lives upon it and within it, to maintain its structure. If any part of these things should fail, in a very great extent of failure, if there were absolutely nothing upon its surface, not even an ocean, then it would indeed become obsolete. It would, to all intents and purposes, die, because the Earth depends not only on all those energy forces which surround it from every source, but also on that which lives upon it, feeds from it and thereby returns and gives to it.

Q: So as an intelligence, the Earth can feel a love force from man.

M: Most definitely. One of the very important aspects of our work with our group and all people who come toward us, whether in the group or beyond it, is that they should love their Earth, that they should send rhythmic impulses toward it, through words of power, through the AUM, through healing energies. Without this, which has been taking place over many years in a very solid and very energetic form, the Earth would have suffered far more greatly by this time than indeed it has.

Q: For those people here who've read about Atlantis, was the destruction of Atlantis brought about by the lack of love shown by man toward his Earth?

M: That was brought about rather more by the love of power, the desire within part of humanity to rule over the rest of humankind, to bring about more and more for themselves, that really started the destruction. Then of course, once this had begun to take place, a whole new spiral of events began, whereby it was very difficult for good to rise above the evil, or good energy to rise above the negative, and it was far easier to draw a line across what was taking place and allow a renewal in a very small way with those that would be aware of the Earth's needs and build upon this. Therefore there were some that survived and moved to other lands, other countries and began their life there, slowly but surely their civilisation was renewed, survived and continued. It wasn't a complete death of the Earth; if that had occurred no one would be here now, and nor would I, two thousand years ago, have been able to welcome a very important and very beautiful energy into the circumstance of the Earth around where I lived.

So a complete knowledge of God and what is beyond God was able to commence at that time and of course from time to time, sometimes with a few thousand years between, sometimes much longer, certain energies can be planted into the Earth which bring about a complete change, a true awakening of energy that man can learn from and everything that depends upon the earth can begin to grow into and develop.

Reply: So the incarnating soul has an awareness of its effect upon the earth at a Higher Self level?

M: Always.

Reply: But the personality that we adopt has the free will to listen to that or not?

M: Absolutely.

Reply: So we, as we know, have the future of the planet entirely in our hands?

M: Again, absolutely.

Q: *Master, I'm just trying to link what you have just been talking about and the excellent questions that have been asked. I'm trying to link the pathway of the soul with our conduct upon the earth and our use of free will. It seems to me that the earth and the soul of man have a relationship and that what we do when we incarnate is that we attempt in some way to raise our vibrational levels, either on an emotional or an intellectual level, in order to be able to enhance the vibrational qualities of our soul. What can we as incarnating human beings do on a practical level to enhance the pathway of the soul?*

M: You can acknowledge initially that your bodies are comprised of exactly the same energy forces and units as the earth itself. You are part of the earth on which you live, the same structure.Water is very important for your earth to survive and you are mostly water. It is similar with the crystals, the crystals deep within the earth which come through to the very surface are important for the Earth's survival and they are also important for the survival of humanity. Earth's intelligence, linked with its other planetary forces, also has a link with humanity. Think of how the Earth conforms absolutely to its rhythm of the seasons, if man is going to survive he has to follow this through also. If you are in a country where the temperature is sub-zero, you are hardly likely to walk out as though it is a summer's day; so you have a linking with everything that is around you, according to comfort, temperature, the availability of food and absolutely everything else. So man and his Earth are one, even if mankind didn't really wish to acknowledge this. If there is intelligence to accept this then surely mankind has to realise that if he neglects what is his means of living he is not going to continue to live. If he does not plant, if he does not reap what he has sown, then he cannot benefit from it by being able to feed his body and allowing it to survive from its most important dietary process. The nutrients that go into the earth are important to the earth and the nutrients it yields are important to humanity.

So these are virtually basic requirements which are acknowledged, whether it is by a primitive society that knows little beyond this, or whether it is in a society that has recognised that life beyond the basic is just as important for progress as the very primitive life was to man a million years before. We have talked at other times of the progress of man and how he should move through time, absorbing change, absorbing what creation has allowed him to accept and to learn from and to give back to creation. The soul recognises that if it does not comply with certain rules and regulations brought about by the habitat of Earth, it cannot feed back to the Higher Self what has been learned within the life. To sit in a darkened room, to be fed through a small hole, is not living it is existing and there are very few people who can do this for very long and in whatever circumstances without losing the ability to think, to move and even to breathe. There is always something that determines man's ability to exist and move on. Does this answer your question, my son?

Reply: I think in part. I was also wondering whether there is a quality of awareness, a vibrational level of thought man also develops through his experience of life on Earth and the exercise of the free will enables you to hone that, so that it becomes a much more powerful process as the soul develops?

M: It is not so much the power of thought as the improving of the instinct within which enables progress to take place. We might say that man is two parts, or three parts instinct and one part intelligence, which enables him to use his instinct in a much more powerful way, but that one part is equally important as the instinct, because it enables man to rise above the level of the animal world in order to survive in extreme conditions which an animal could not. Where the Earth itself is concerned, it is virtually at a level of survival that unless something interferes, unless something that man creates causes devastation to such an extent that the Earth is placed off its course, or is devastated and is no longer able to function in the correct way, then the Earth's dependence upon man is of course there. It is dependent upon nature, vegetation, as well as upon the energies fed to it from the seven spheres of light that surround it and are part of its own energy field.

Perhaps in our next talk we could elaborate a little upon this, upon the dependence within the Earth on these spheres, although it would only take up a small part of our talk. We are beginning to see how your minds are working and maybe it is a time when we should give a little more enlightenment on this.

Q: If a god or an angel chooses to take a body and come to the Earth, can it generate karma and will it need to return again, or is it only mankind that does that through his inferiority to these other soul beings?

M: Can we remove the word 'inferiority' because in this instance it is because the angel, for example, or the very high spiritual teacher, shall we say a being like Yeshua, comes with the entire Higher Self within that human structure, so there is no need for reincarnation or karma, because it has all been assuaged. The second part of your question as to why man needs to come repeatedly in order to understand karma and to clear it, is from the choice of man so to do. The Higher Self realises how important man is to the Earth, indeed to all the spheres of progress and so gives that opportunity, but once man has reached a certain pinnacle of knowledge then another aspect does not return. Although the Angels of Light and the very highly aware spiritual teachers have not come through a process as rigid as man, there is still that acknowledgment that the intelligence and the love that is stored within his Higher Self is of importance to the Earth's progress and he will seek one way or another to ensure that it is reflected within mankind, so that the Earth's ability to continue and to grow cannot be impeded.

We thank you so much for your interest, my children. Do continue to make notes of those things that we have not made clear to you, and in the next three sessions that we will have with you we will try and clear up the rest of this soul riddle. Maybe in the last one we could have a united endeavour to have lots of questions on the subject – that which has been covered and that which has not.

Until we meet again, our love surround you as you grow in your desire for knowledge and grow also in your desire for peace. Shalom.

The Spheres of Light

The following discussion is part of a private session that one of the group members had with the Master. It is included here at the Master's request.

Master: We will speak on the spheres of light and their purposes. There are seven. Each one is individual within itself for the purpose for which it has been created, but each merges into the other, either moving outward from the Earth itself or moving inward commencing from the Christos. For the purposes of this discussion we will start with the Earth. The Earth itself and that of which you are well aware do not need to be explained further at this moment. You are part of its rhythm and yet you are also part of the rhythm of the seven spheres which merge from it and go forward through time and space. All of those spheres are within yourself, rotating within their rhythm and forming part of your life, your prospects, your health, well-being, the ageing process and everything that moves ultimately towards the cessation of personality and bodily life and merging into spirit.

The first sphere that man finds himself dwelling in after death is the green sphere. It is so known and so called because it is closest to Earth, which is very largely also green. It is a replica of the Earth, it is the etheric of the Earth. It is a band of colour of light that emerges from deep within the Earth's boundaries within the different bands which have come about for the several million years that Earth has been in existence. As the spirit of mankind moves away from the Earth's sphere into the etheric it needs, there are so many things which it would expect to be there, which would not, to quote man's vernacular these days, 'faze him'. When his eyes are closed in death and opened in spirit, that which is familiar surrounds him. You might say, 'If that is so, how do we know we have died, how do we not think that we are perhaps dreaming?' Usually it is because there are people present whom we know within ourselves have passed over. We do not see the companions of life, we see instead those that we have loved who have gone before, some of them many, many years before, some whom we recognise and yet have not seen, those from a past age, those from a past life. There is something within the soul aspect that recognises, that knows who they are. Everything else is so very similar to the Earth – the trees, the grass – but what is different is the sky above. It is no longer with its infinite colours representing clouds, sunshine, the moon, stars. That belongs to Earth, it does not belong to the spirit spheres. What you see around you is almost an eerie stillness, a gentle light that never changes. It is a light that both invigorates and yet also provides peace. Many refer to it as the sepia light and yet things shine forth within that light – there is no wind, no rain, no elements of any sort to destroy that in which you find yourself. There is no heat or cold and you are aware within this light that you also have an ability to move as never before. You do not need your limbs on which to walk and yet they are there. The whole of your body is as you remember it and yet as you move across the Earth you glide. The spirit body quickly acclimatises to this, becomes aware also that with the speed of thought you can be wherever you desire to be with whomsoever you please.

Q: Would that mean that you could only access those in the same sphere or those in a higher sphere as well?

M: Those from higher spheres can merge into a lower sphere without any problem at all and generally come when bidden. Those that you wish to communicate with upon the Earth, their soul, their etheric being while they live can indeed be called upon and will come during the hours of sleep, the hours of rest and the communication takes place. If you as a spirit being desire to penetrate into the Earth, that is far more difficult. In fact it is usually from the higher planes with those who have a greater understanding of the merging of spirit and of moving through the density of the Earth that can achieve this rather than those that have just entered the spirit realm. There are exceptions, there is always an exception to every rule, but in general it is very difficult and therefore it is not embarked upon by the new spirit.

Q: At the point of death, does the rhythm of the soul change?

M: Yes. It becomes much faster, very much more vibrant.

Q: So all we are actually doing is remaining in the same place and the higher rhythm gives you a completely different outlook?

M: Yes, that is a very good explanation of what takes place.

Q: So the spheres of light that radiate from the Earth are actually all part of each of the seven spheres and are in the same place at the same time. It is the soul's speed of vibration that carries you forward and helps you progress?

M: That is very largely right. There is also a response within each of those spheres represented by their bands of colour which denotes what takes place in that sphere. After a while when the etheric has accepted the passage of time, the passage of death, and has gone through the sense of accepting what lessons have been learned and what are still to be learned, it goes through the Akashic and accepts that another aspect from within the Higher Self, if not already upon the Earth would indeed need to travel there, attain a body and attain the awareness of what is still needed to be learned. Of course from that particular awareness the soul can travel to where the Higher Self is congregated with all its knowledge, share what has taken place within the Earth's perimeter, see which aspect it feels will understand most greatly the next stage of development and even assess its need to be on its way and how to help it adjust initially to the Earth's vibration. We cannot measure this in time as we do not have it.

The pink and yellow spheres
From that point we move into the second sphere. This is known generally as the pink sphere – green brings balance, pink brings harmony. Not only is there harmony in the second sphere, because adjustments have been made and understanding of what has been achieved during the Earth's sojourn, but also there is a more peaceful awareness within the soul, a greater awareness of what lies ahead. Pink is also the colour of compassion; compassion is very much an earthly attribute. It is of the personality, it is something which grows through the use and the understanding of how to deal with other members of humanity. As it is also highlighted within the pink colour it is part of that awareness of the soul as it moves into the second sphere. Within that sphere there are further developments of knowledge, there is the availability of the halls of light, the halls of learning. There is the ability to speak with those teachers that perhaps you have become aware of during your earthly life and

they are there present within their spirit form, their spirit light, to be able to give further direction, further teaching. So although it is the second sphere for the soul, it is the first of the enlightenment spheres. Now there are many aspects of soul that quite truly never move beyond the green sphere, because they cannot grasp what it is they have been in life for and until that is grasped the etheric cannot move on to the pink sphere, lose the etheric body and begin to vibrate as spirit. So those that do [grasp the purpose of their life] are already commencing their journey of enlightenment.

Q: So those that remain within the green sphere that travel to the Akashic record, they are searching for the reason for life so that they can then take that up to another aspect and assist it to come back. If they cannot accept the basic premise of their existence and yet the Higher Self is aware of that purpose on Earth why, when you are in the green sphere, does that awareness not re-visit you?

M: You might not be prepared for it, you might not yet be ready to assimilate it. If you look at your progress while you are on Earth you have certain interests, you have a certain mental ability. You have those things that can be assimilated that you desire to do or appertain to do. It is possible that there are many reasons you cannot go forward to greater understanding. Whether it is something within the Earth like learning chemistry or learning philosophy, you may not have the right equipment within yourself to learn this. So it is the same as an aspect dwelling within the body. The aspect returning to the Higher Self fulfils its own designation, fulfils its own path, but it cannot move into the path of another – it has already completed it while it is in the body.

Q: Then in that first sphere, if it has completed its path on Earth, when it reaches that sphere upon death, surely it is aware that it has achieved its purpose?

M: Indeed, yes.

Q: Then why would it remain there not accepting it?

M: It doesn't necessarily remain there for the rest of existence but it may remain there a great deal longer than another aspect that has achieved more, that has more spiritual awareness, which can move on very quickly, in some cases skip that sphere altogether and find itself on awakening within the pink sphere with the further enlightenment available to it.

Q: Are the higher spheres there to assist and teach the lower?

M: Always, up to the point of the violet and amethyst spheres which merge together. The one which follows the pink sphere is the yellow and that is the first sphere of the mind. Still there is the availability of the knowledge from the Earth which is being assimilated into the first two spheres, the pink and the green, also preparing the soul for further spiritual enlightenment that it has begun to seek on the Earth but is now there, with all its certainty, with the enlightenment that cannot change, that is acceptable to the God force and which emanated from God. So that yellow sphere we call one of enlightenment for the soul itself.

The blue, violet and amethyst spheres
Beyond this, going into the higher spheres you have those that have achieved enlightenment, possibly through hundreds and thousands of incarnations. Many of those that have already achieved a complete understanding within the Higher Self that no longer wish to send an aspect to the Earth dwell within this particular sphere which is the sphere of mind and is the blue sphere. Here you find the masters and teachers, you find those that come through inspiration and also make themselves known through meditation. The Higher Self dwells very largely within the blue sphere; it is a sphere of intelligence, a sphere that those upon Earth benefit very greatly from when they are wishing for inspiration to develop their work, develop their spiritual acumen. At this point we will go quite quickly through the spheres and then come back to any questions you have for us.

Beyond the blue sphere is the violet and amethyst sphere. The teachers of light and the masters that have reached a certain understanding of their designated work dwell within their total Higher Self in that sphere. It is from that sphere that Master Joseph can speak with you. He and many other spiritual teachers that dwell upon that sphere of light achieve the ability to go through these different-coloured spheres, the different energy levels, the different vibrations. They are able to move through the very heavy vibration that surrounds the Earth in order to be able to give voice to their knowledge, give voice to their teaching. There are comparatively few that can actually mingle with their mediums, their channellers, to do this. There are many who can come close through thought. As the vibrations move through the different spheres the thoughts can amalgamate with those of human beings, which leads to the kind of teaching which comes through inspiration. That which comes through the presence of the teacher to allow those present with the channeller maybe to see the vibration of the Teacher, to feel it, to be aware of the colours that surround them, everything of course depending upon that human-cum-spiritual awareness within the individual, is because the spiritual teacher is able to bring a vibration into the earthly world which can be picked up, seen or felt, as the case may be, through those that are present.

The Master's form of channelling

In our own case it is as though we were seated within the centre of the child through whom we speak – she becomes us and we become her. When we separate, when we move away in order to return to our sphere, it is felt as a moving energy within herself, a feeling initially of rejection. Sometimes we are able to hold more closely to her when she has finished channelling to enable her without speech, without vibration, simply still, to be aware of that stillness and peace, that quality which comes from those of that sphere, which is very, very important to her to recognise and to be familiar with the teacher she has been sharing with her audience. So that particular sphere, the sphere of the mind, is all important for direction, for bringing the spiritual aspirations of man into harmony and unity, for allowing mankind to be aware that there is something which is beyond religious principle which is indeed usually man's first awareness of the God force.

The golden sphere

Now that which lies beyond the amethyst sphere is not accessible to anything other than the divine. There is no possibility of coming within the radius of humanity in the same vibration as the masters and teachers are able to do through the deeper form of channelling. In some of humanity an inspiration can still come into their lives, usually through a very deep form of meditation, perhaps the Transcendental Meditation. Maybe those who dedicate their lives to the spiritual understanding of those spheres, who barely resonate to human echoes, to human feelings, they can be assimilated into the vibration of that sphere which is the golden sphere. What lies beyond that is the God force, the Christos. It manifests in the clearest, pearliest light, the light of all eternity, the light of creation, a bright crystal light. It is as though there were a crystal of the rarest proportions suspended in eternity, turning gently, emitting its light through all its facets. It is this that gradually is assimilated by all the spheres, giving creation into the colours, into the energies that pass from one to another including also the Earth as it manifests its growth and its ability to remain constant within the universe itself. So those are the seven spheres and those are the approximate areas of growth within each one that the spirit of man, the soul of man, aspires to.

Q: Why would a being on Earth wish to dedicate himself so much towards the spiritual life that they will achieve when they go into those realms anyway? Is that part of what their reason is for coming to Earth?

M: Most definitely. If the Higher Self wishes to aspire to being conscious of the God force in its individual state then it will, of course, encourage one or more of its aspects to reach towards this. You have to remember that once you get into the golden light and the crystal light you are no longer individual with the ability to resonate individually with thought. You are part of the whole, you are part as we have mentioned before, of the still quiet pool of knowledge but unable to resonate your own quality of knowledge within it – you are immersed. You are part of the life force.

Q: If you, from your current amethyst sphere, moved up to the golden sphere then we would not be able to have this conversation through your channel?

M: Absolutely. But we have pledged that this will not happen while our child is here upon the Earth and is willing to allow us to use her vibration in order to teach.

Q: Is it true then, that your Higher Self is complete and vibrates with no aspect anywhere other than in that single vibration?

M: It is true.

Q: The other teachers that are around you, that your channel also channels, Father Abraham and the Prophet Elijah, they are equally individual Higher Selves, complete, but you are ready to move into the next sphere should you desire to move and become part of the golden sphere?

M: That is so. It is as though a doorway would open and in the mists of that light, which is a living light, a living vibration, when the call comes we cannot resist it. The main reason that teachers such as Abraham and Elijah, Moses and many others of the great prophesiers and teachers of ancient times are still able to contact the Earth is the knowledge that within this particular age such changes will take place that will need profound guidance. Therefore those teachers that have been prepared for this – and it has taken many thousands of years to allow them to become progressively aware of the needs of man, how to contact man and how to guide him forward in such a way that he can understand – once this task is done the Earth will have progressed to such an extent that that kind of teaching, that kind of channelling will no longer be apposite and therefore those many teachers will go forward and will become part of the living essence from which all life emerged.

Chapter 4

Talk Four, February

The link between soul and personality. Colour, chakras and personalities. Bliss. The purpose of God. The Children of Light. The purpose of the planets. Ego and soul. The power of God and the free will of man. The nature of Christ.

Master: My children, shalom and welcome! There was a slight problem this day deciding which of the subjects we should embark upon, because there is still quite a procedure to talk through and to discuss. So we thought that on this occasion we would commence by asking you your questions and possibly enlarging upon these as we review what is already taught and what we feel is already absorbed, so initially at least we will do this. So we will leave it to you, as usual, to indicate which of those present should ask questions, so that everyone does not speak together. Remember that the talk, as always, is regarding the soul, its development, its journey and all things appertaining to the soul, but not necessarily to other teachings that we will embark upon at another time. So speak on.

Q: You've said in the past that the soul is here to learn from all sorts of situations and experiences, both positive and negative. My concern is how the soul is able to direct the personality and also I'm thinking of particularly vicious or brutal dictators. I can't really believe that the amount of violence and pain inflicted is necessary for the soul's learning; so if we take that sort of scenario, what is going on there? Is the soul failing to connect with the personality in some way? Of course there are many people who deny the soul, deny even the existence of it.

M: We agree, mainly that is because it cannot be seen or felt in connection with the body, although at times to try and bring a little awareness to people of the situation of the soul we have discussed it as being within every cell of the body, for example, and not in any particular cell or organ, in the real truth of the matter it is within the aura and it is within the 'joining,' as it were, of personality with Higher Self in all the degrees of the 'spheres,' although that word is not strictly accurate. Around your body you do have something very similar to the spheres that surround your Earth. They are circles of light, they lessen and deepen according to the reality that your soul brings to your personality. All of you, we are sure, know of what you refer to as 'very shallow people.' They seem to have very little in the way of desire to express anything, to learn anything, to realise either a religion or a spirituality within themselves. They just go on from day to day expressing their anger, their disbelief, whatever their emotion may be. So it is almost a circle of emotions that are encircling the human frame until eventually that circle has extended into the spheres of light themselves, thus co-ordinating the ability of the Higher Self to merge into the personality, guiding it and also in some respects being guided by it.

Now all of these things are important to know, to accept within yourself that although they cannot be seen or touched or felt in any way at all, that they are there. You don't have to see the blood flowing around your body to know that is what it's doing. You don't have to feel your heart beating to know its purpose, to know it is keeping you alive. You don't have to open your eyes in the darkness to see, to know, that there are objects that are there very clearly when your eyes are open, or when the darkness has moved into daylight. So there are certain things that you accept and one of these is that the Higher Self is the motivation for all the actions that take place while you are in life and that if this were not so, mankind would be purely an automaton that moved around utterly selfishly, unaware of the needs and concerns of others, simply doing what it has to do to exist. It is the soul, the rhythm of life itself within that soul, that enables humanity to be the strongest of the animals within the kingdom of Earth.

Q: In previous talks you have spoken about how different personalities are governed by different auric colours. I can see that there are similarities in the meaning of these colours whether they are in the spheres or within the individual. In your discussion on the spheres there is quite a lot about green and pink, but not so much when you come to the rest of the spectrum. Could you say a little about how the colours affect different personalities?

M: It does not so much affect an individual's personality but their purpose in coming into life, in the areas they are born, to the parents that they have chosen, and also to the initial and overriding purpose of the Higher Self itself. A blue spectrum personality, as we have explained many times, rather rules the intellect more than the heart, but of course they have their purpose in life, it is very important. It is also important that with all the colours in the spectrum, each one begins to blossom into something other than that which they initially accepted as their task.

Ideally all mankind should begin to look toward the spiritual in their development and in their handling of life, but so often those who are born within the blue ray, or who seem to have rather stuck in that channel through their lives, will often not develop the really spiritual aspect within that life. It is almost as though they feel that by showing gentleness, tenderness, compassion, that they are giving away something that is integral within themselves as to the showing of their intellect, their ability to shine – either, as is often the case, those who teach or those who have positions of authority – and feel that to show they are able to have compassion for the situation, for others, would reduce the amount of respect or authority that they have gained. So the blue spectrum is the very challenging one. It needs a great deal of help, a great deal of upliftment and when those within it begin to soften, they begin to recognise that just to earn respect, just to be admired for what they can produce, does not allow them to feel at one with society and humanity in the same way as those who have a somewhat gentler sign and rather softer colour.

Where the greens are concerned, they do bring a balance. They seem to be able to liaise with both those moving more toward the blue – and remember that the turquoises and other shades of blue also come into the equation, and sometimes those that are a very clear, stark blue will begin to modulate their colours and will become much softer, rather more of a bluey-green. In all of these colours there are degrees, from the very softest, palest, to the richest and deepest. If you think to yourself that with all those divisions of colours there is the infinite variety that mankind finds within his life, within his friendships and his work, then we feel you can sort out for yourself just how wide the spectrum is and how beautiful the variety of understanding coming forth within mankind. But interesting as that question is, we covered it in its bare bones, shall we say, and we have not entered a little more deeply into it. If this doesn't truly satisfy, then maybe on the last occasion we can go over all these 'not quite assimilated' aspects and truly round them off.

The soul of animals

There are other animals that have a very, very gentle nature, extremely so, so we cannot say that the soul is only in humankind. There is a soul that is within animalkind, but it vibrates very differently because animals all have their purpose. If you look at some animals, what seems to be uppermost is self-preservation and if you look at some human beings you see the same trait – they must preserve themselves, whatever any others may be doing; but the ability of the Higher Self to resonate within depends absolutely upon man's degree of growth, and his own awareness of his ability to render to others what he would do to himself.

The reason why there are all of these lives is the very gradual progress forward, not everyone has reached the same degree of lifetimes as others. The Higher Self may have been diligent in its progression, or it may not even have needed to progress to that extent, so you get a much more selfish, antagonistic, brutal person who has not had the experience of the many lives of learning how to modulate themselves, how to become more compassionate. So those such as the personalities you mentioned, my son, you can accept that they have not come into many lives that have brought the gentleness to the fore. They have a great deal of selfishness within them, the desire is there to dominate. To this present day there are those in the public eye, very often they choose such occupations as sport, because this enables them to express their need to be strong or to dominate.

Dominance and sport

There are those sports of course which are absolutely sharing and which are true sports from that understanding, but there are also those which allow the dominance and sometimes the cruelty to come forward, which is a satisfaction to the personality. It always goes back to the fact that the incarnating soul has reached a particular stage of its development, and that life is an opportunity to overcome that trait, to allow more gentleness to develop, in the same way as those that are born sick or crippled, be it mentally or physically. It is not a life of punishment, as has been mooted to us recently, it is a life of opportunity to overcome that sense of non-achievement, so it also applies to those with very low self-esteem. The life they are in gives them opportunities to recognise themselves, their worth and what they can achieve. Even those with little, if any, intelligence because of brain damage, or being born with a damaged brain – there are always things that the soul and the personality can achieve, however little it may be and very often those who are very severely crippled indeed are so gentle, so loving, so utterly unselfish that they can but only create a feeling of compassion and tenderness toward them.

So those that are using brute force within their lives for their achievements, when they go back to the Higher Self they are faced with the reality of what they have done. They are faced not just with the reaction but with the results of the action and that can be far more brutal to the non-achiever than any feeling of success they might feel within themselves through being powerful or great. No soul gets away with murder, my children, because very simply they see what has taken place to all those involved, the loved ones, the dependents, on and on and on, not just that action of anger or fear, but the repercussions of that action in both the person killed and those around them.

Q: Our little son who has recently been born – I've been observing and connecting with him. When he was first born he appeared to be very much in bliss and very soon afterwards he began to reach out and you can see now that he is beginning to take things in, beginning to experience what actually is around him. I saw in this something you said in your last talk, that somehow the Absolute was in bliss – the creative power of the Godhead – and yet wanted to experience. Although I watched my son doing this and wondered why he bothered to come out of bliss when after all we are all seeking this bliss, I wonder if you can explain more about why there is this need for the Godhead, the Absolute, the Creative Power, to have to experience what is after all in many cases suffering, when It already has complete bliss?

M: If you had that state of bliss, if you entered into it and you were able to shut out everything else within your life, would you want to return to anything of a lesser state of being? Of course you wouldn't! But how else would you learn? If you only experienced the ultimate, you would do nothing that would either help you to understand that bliss and how to achieve it, nor yet the most important lesson within life, of assisting another to achieve it. If you see whatever your vision of a soul may be, all nicely tucked up in a pink cloud, bobbing away, thoroughly enjoying that state, not one of these little clouds touching another, all very, very selfishly content within themselves, how would the reason for entering a life, the reason for becoming part of existence ever shape up? It needs one cloud to bump into the other, giving a little jolt, so that at least they realise what it is like for an impact to take place – and you could call birth an impact, initially – to realise you are not on your own within this state, that there is something else out there; and then the imagination begins to work and the soul begins to think, 'There is somebody else enjoying what I am enjoying. I do hope they are not enjoying more than I am,' and then off they go and they will say, 'Hey there! Are you enjoying absolutely the same as me and if so, why so?' We may sound a little frivolous, but it does illustrate the point we wish to make, that coming into life is a communal effect, it is not just for one soul on its own to experience. These young souls coming into flesh, that have never been before within that personality, within that flesh, they have to gradually, gently acclimatise themselves to human beings, to actions, to noise, whatever it might be and they should not be protected from these things, otherwise they become very, very selfish. But we do not deny them that little return to what they remember, so young they cannot remember anything taking place around them between those things taking place. Gradually they begin to associate hunger with a need for food, the approach of food, however it takes place, as a quenching of that hunger and they go forward like that.

Reply: *Master, the real question behind that was why the Godhead Itself had to experience when It had Its own bliss?*

M: For the same reason, virtually, that It was so content with the knowledge of everything that was beautiful, everything that had been created within an image of love, because the Godhead is the love image. It realised from Its own intelligence, from Its own capacity of reasoning, that whatever else there might be extending beyond that bliss of love could maybe be controlled by the love itself – and it can. Love is all-forgiving, love can bring everything into a state of awareness, even the most harsh, the cruellest within the world, if shown love can cry. So the Godhead is not outside of these emotions; the Godhead is the Ultimate Emotion and in creating an image that is very similar to Itself, an image that is an energy force that at the same time creates, keeps alive, develops, allows all the emotions necessary within life to take place, then that Godhead is true fatherhood and when in life we become fathers or mothers, we are then expressing what the Godhead within Itself also expresses in seeing the existence of man, the pride as well as the sadness and knowing that within that expression there is always hope for man. Give him enough opportunities, let him come back often enough, let him see what other species of mankind have done to his Earth and perhaps he will learn from this and try to create something more beautiful and more peaceful.

Q: Could you say something about the connection between genetics and light streams. For example someone born to a Child of Light* who isn't a Child of Light, what do they inherit physically and spiritually? How could those born in the early Egyptian dynasties link back into the genetic materials necessary to carry on that knowledge if an aspect comes back into life today?

M: The answer to that, of course, is not simple – it cannot be. A few words cannot describe to those who wish to work out possibly their own genetic stream, without again having to accept a formation, a 'drawing' shall we say. That drawing would be very complex indeed. You would need to have, as scientists have, an awareness, understanding of all the atomic structures that are in existence. Very possibly if algebra was used to describe it, it would cover an area the size of the country in which you are now living. It is that complex, that difficult to comprehend and yet the soul itself can, with the flash of the eye, move into whatever division of those atoms that it wishes, linking up absolutely with what it needs to remember, what it needs to change, even creating in the past what was not then achieved in order to bring an achievement into the present; and why? Because it is right outside of the comprehension of man – the past, present and future encapsulated in the now.

*The Children of Light are very old souls who have no further need to incarnate. They have voluntarily agreed to be born at this time in order to help the transition of humanity into the Golden Age. They are highly intuitive with a deep sense of purpose and are distinguished from the rest of humankind by having no karma. There are two streams of these children; those who had their major incarnations during the time of Atlantis and those who lived important spiritual lives during the Egyptian dynasties. The eldest are currently in their late teens. For a full description read the Monograph entitled 'The Children of Light' by Father Abraham.

Past and future in the now

Whatever we say, however we try to enable people to understand, we fall short in words, in actions, in any way at all, to
allow man to understand that complexity. Can everything be
now, at this moment and yet we take seventy or eighty years to
get through it, and a past aspect has taken twenty or thirty, and
we go back a hundred thousand lives, all now, all at this second
in time? And all we can say is yes! Probably man's computer, his
brain, as it expands and grows through all the years, depending
upon which light stream he is born into, can eventually work
out that all-embracing at-one-ness with the now.

The nearest anyone ever gets to it is in meditation, when
the mind flows freely into the whole cosmos, where there is
nothing that binds it to that moment that was left when the
meditation began; and yet there is something which says,
'You've had your time now, come back to reality, come back to
the Earth and continue with your life.' To try and recapture
those brief moments of floating, of moving, of being and of
feeling, you can never do it, because the next time you enter
into that bliss state you are aware of something else. But have
you gone back in the past to re-achieve it, have you moved into
the future in order to begin it, to mould it, to allow it to be
there when you reach that time in your spectrum of years, will
you then again remember, 'Ah, I was here, I did this, I felt that,
I moved into this?' No, because so much else will have happened that you cannot recall that moment, it has gone; but that
moment is the one moment which will shape your existence
spiritually. It is that one moment where your soul enters, totally
content that it no longer needs to struggle to allow you to
expand and grow. You have achieved it, you are there within it
and if everyone stayed within that you wouldn't need a past,
present and future, because all the God-knowledge that you are
seeking is there in that moment.

We are sorry that we cannot explain more finitely to you,
but if you can imagine the interlinking of your complete genetic
system in that way and just trust, my children, trust that the
overriding principle of your Higher Self and the soul guiding
you will achieve what it desires to achieve in the span of your
years, then you can stop worrying about it. You can begin to
enjoy it, you can say that 'this session is part of six; in each one
I will learn something,' and it will slot away in the brain and in
the mind. Remember it is the mind that achieves your spiritual

growth, not the brain. The brain is the human side of you. When that is dead, you are dead and you cannot be brought back again, but your mind never dies, your mind will return into its greater whole and all will be clear. You might look back, you might see yourself in your last resting place – most souls do and then they lose interest – but that moment might be, 'He achieved so little, he was foolish, he expected too much.'

Q: I wanted to ask about the relationship between the ego structure, the personality and how frequently it is very blocking toward the soul's expression.

M: That is, of course, very true. The more aware a person becomes spiritually, the more accepting they are that they must let that ego take second place and that the knowledge they are learning of a spiritual nature can far surpass that which they are learning on a physical basis, or even scholastically. It has its place, but the ego can insist that it is all-important, that the spiritual is not really necessary and clutters up the space which is being given to improving the status in life or proving to another that you know more than they do and therefore they are inferior. Many people indulge themselves in an ego trip in that way. However, as the spiritual develops, the person can then say to themselves, 'I know a great deal about A, B and C, but I must accept that others may know more than I do about E, F and G and I can learn from them and have a much wider spectrum of knowledge which will make conversation interesting, which will make teaching another a task which will be enjoyable to both.' So the ego is part of the personality, but it doesn't have to rule it. It should indeed be ruled by the incarnating facet of soul that is desiring to learn and achieve within the present life. In fact, my child, anyone who recognises that their ego is a stumbling block is already two-thirds upon the route to overcoming that and to saying to themselves, 'I must control this and recognise that being egotistical is preventing me from learning my spiritual lessons.'

Reply: Is there anything that can dispel or lessen the impact of the ego structure?

M: The best thing is knowledge. Most people do not have to express their own ego if they have a great deal of knowledge about the subject that they wish to share. It is usually lack of knowledge which encourages the ego to shout loudly, so that people have to listen either because of the personality or the bombastic way that the knowledge is being shared. It is the kind of attitude of, 'It's no good arguing with me, I won't listen to arguments, I know it all already. Whatever you know is inferior to my knowledge.' Everybody thinks, 'Oh, that person must know a great deal about that subject, look at how demeaning he is of those professors, of those people who have spent all their lives studying and becoming well-known in their field. Look at him, he must be the greatest.' Then along comes a wise one and the wise one sits there very quietly, very gently, very interested in what the egotist wishes to say, and the questions are a little more searching, a little more progressive and the egotist begins to squirm a little, begins to wish that the conversation would end, because they realise how little they really know; and usually the wise one will say, 'Ah yes, but you have stopped learning, you have stopped being a student.' Those who continue to be students all their lives are truly wise and they lose their ego, so if you bear that in mind and when in doubt, when you feel you want your ego to express your knowledge, remain quiet and listen to what others wish to express, then you may learn something. That goes for all of you!

Q: Master, in a private session recently you told me that all the planetary life [non-human life forms in the universe] *is actually very dull and that only on Earth is there this sort of existence with an emotional quality to it. I need a little clarification about this. Does planetary life incarnate from our Higher Selves, or are there some other Higher Selves in other evolutions that are not connected? Are we just earthbound, or do we have aspects on the planetary life as well?*

M: No, you don't have soul aspects on the planets. They are a completely different structure from that which dwells upon the Earth. As we have explained in other teachings, which no doubt can be called upon for clarification here, they have been designed as a support for the Earth plane – the Earth itself, of course, being a planet, but being specifically created for humankind to develop and learn. The planets have their own intelligence, they have their own life, but there is no form upon the planets; it is an intelligence which links with the Earth plane, with the planet that is called Earth, or the world, and helps it within its ability to develop, grow and sustain life for man. Without the energy fields which come forth from the planets the Earth could well simply decline and die, and so would mankind. So the whole object of creating an existence for man that produces harmony and also produces knowledge regarding his own home, his own planet, and all the rest of the universe, could not be achieved, it would not go forward.

Man has reached that point now in his intelligence that he is exploring the planetary life, as he does this more and more closely, he is learning that its composition is very different from his own Earth, and he has not yet discovered the link between a planet and the Earth to his own satisfaction. He is still looking for the more fundamental things that link the Earth with himself, but over a period of time, possibly several more hundreds of years, this will become more clarified, especially as he produces those instruments which examine the planets much more closely and even are enabled to travel there, in the same way as they have placed man upon the moon. But the colourlessness of the planets is not quite what we wished to express. They have a colour, a richness of their own, through the harmonies of the spirals of light which encircle them, in the same way as the spirals encircle the Earth, maintaining and supporting the light streams, the spiritual planes, the planes where the Higher Self and its aspects can travel, attaining the specific knowledge that earthly beings are here to create and learn from, eventually perhaps to be able to harmonise more with the specific life forms, or energy forms, which are attached to the planetary life. As man begins to find a link between the energies of the planets and his own planet, things will become a lot more clear to him than they are at the present time.

The advantages of Earth

When you look at the planets through your instruments, with some you can see beautiful colours and a cadence of light which make you feel you wish to travel there and be part of them, but you are actually looking through your own spectrum, you are looking through that which encircles your planet and which gives it its length, breadth and depth of light that you simply accept when you look at it through your eyes and you see all the magnificent colours. If you were a planetary being you would not see your planet in the same light, in the same way. So mankind has so many things for him that are much more advanced. Even though the planets are millions of years older than the Earth they still do not have the advantages that man has because of man's link with the God energies.

Now the God energies – and we are going over old ground here – the God energies as you know them do not link with the planetary life, but the life that created the universe links with this. So if you look back on your notes from previous talks we have given in this series where we have been talking about the life force of creation, the God force, and then all the dignitaries; the Archangels, the Teachers of Light, and so forth, right down to mankind, you will then see how the structure links with the planets and with the Earth; but that of course is one fraction of what is in other universes and there is no way that we can embark upon that information within six short lectures. We can only say that other universes do exist, they have their own life forms, but none are the same as man.

Q: The positive and negative energies that swirl about us all, do they affect the personality or do they affect the soul?

M: They don't affect the soul, they do affect the personality. The soul can rise above all of this because the soul is in essence spiritual, because of this it doesn't have the same need to experience as humankind experiences, that which is human finds that their emotions are affected by the different kinds of energy which are evoked by actions. So you might say that emotions bring forth actions, actions bring forth either negative or positive energies and then it all goes back again into the same spiral of energy by which man is affected. His soul is right outside the orb of this particular ability to encircle, to allow the self to be affected by those energies. It's a stabilising factor. Without it, we feel, humankind would find it virtually impossible to be able to exist upon his Earth. He would feel far too fragmented, far too taut and possibly angry or frustrated by everything taking place around him; but because he has emotions and intellect and the ability to learn, few things are so frustrating that they cannot be overcome.

Reply: Then as the aspect decides which path it's going to take on its trip to Earth – and you've said before that many have come to experience war – then the soul is choosing a negative time to come into and is it not therefore adding to the pool of negativity that already exists?

M: No, because it comes in with the opportunity of its knowledge gained before to overcome that negativity, hopefully to ensure that the war will end such activities in the future. It seldom does, of course; it simply changes the mode of warfare, usually meaning it becomes more and more intense, more and more devastating as the centuries pass, but at least there are those that have an opportunity to bring a cessation to the violence. If they do not choose it, or if they are unable to perform such an act, they have the free will to take part or not, as the case may be. If they are coerced into taking part because the activities around them do not permit them to run away or ignore them, then it is still a time that they can develop and grow, seeing what is taking place by the violence, seeing how the hatred of others toward each other destroys the peace, destroys the beauty of God's world. Then as they grow, as perhaps they have their children, they can preach the gospel of peace rather than the gospel of more obtained through violence. Most wars stem from this, stem from the few wanting more than it is right to have and not minding that human life and all they have created is destroyed because of that insatiable desire for more wealth, more land, more everything. We hope that this particular age that we are now involved with will be the commencement of the kind of change that man will relish, that he will see offered to him, and work toward that peace, enable others to have their own share, for he himself to delight in his share, and not demand more and more, until eventually the world is destroyed by that one act of violence which can achieve utter destruction, which is atomic warfare.

Reply: Earlier today you said that the type of individual coming to the Earth that would cause that sort of disharmony would be a young soul, one that hadn't had much experience. So is the premise that you are looking toward a more enlightened age where there aren't so many aspects left that haven't experienced that growth?

M: Largely speaking, yes, but as always we have a proviso. There are plenty of very young aspects that could profit from coming to the Earth and learning from what they find there, but this age is one that will bring about more equilibrium because of the nature of the majority of souls which are already being born and growing within the Earth, namely, of course, the Children of Light. As they grow, have their own children, discipline them in a very different way from the young over the last hundred or so years specifically, as they show enlightenment from within their own depths, there will be fewer of those negative souls, if you wish to call them that, that will have the opportunity to create disturbance and devastation. Up to the present time it has been a fairly even balance within humankind between those who desire perfection and those who wish to destroy, but when the balance is a little more toward the perfectionists, toward the spiritually inclined and the knowledgeable members of mankind, there will be less opportunity for death, and along with our other teachings, of course, the world is progressively getting smaller with its land masses – nothing whatsoever to do with man's mind and man's intelligence – but the spiral of activity which constantly takes place within the world itself. So with fewer to inhabit the Earth, there are fewer to destroy what little they have.

Q: My question is about the fact that the progress of mankind seems to be so slow, and the fact that there isn't more intervention on some level to speed things up.

M: What sort of intervention would you visualise, from where?

Reply: From the God force, basically to lessen the negative effects that are going on and to open people's minds up further, or somehow break through the barriers of the ego structures and the personality structures that create the disharmony and all the other problems that come with it.

M: What makes you think that the God force has that power?

Reply: What about the Children of Light then – wasn't that a choice made, seeing what the Earth was going through?

M: Indeed, but the Children of Light have dwelling within them their entire Higher Self, which has learned through all the hundreds and thousands of lives and has gained from that knowledge, has developed, so that given the opportunity they can break through all these limitations and allow the Earth a much better chance of survival. This is why they are here, but the God force can do nothing. The God force has not incarnated into flesh, with activities that can either make or mar what is happening; the God force is an energy which allows all things within the universe to work according to law. It is only man, through his free will, who works outside of the law, thus creating havoc. God didn't create havoc, God created a most beautiful structure upon which man eventually was given the opportunity to live. He cannot, if you wish to use the intimate term of He – we would rather say It, create action. The God force can only provide the ability for the action to take place. We know it is a very difficult subject to accept. Always we come back to little limitations which we truly understand, but that is mainly because the nature of the universe, the nature of the God force and of the Universal Creator is still not fully understood and accepted by humankind. Once its truth is assimilated then people will not consider God to blame for death, destruction, be it a child who has died or a country that has been devastated. They will then begin to recognise that it is that ultimate gift, free will, which is responsible for everything, good and evil, positive and negative that occurs. It all has its own structure, it all has its cause and effect. Not God, but man.

Q: Wasn't the Christ an intervention then, Master?

M: He was indeed an intervention which worked partially, and hopefully may work even more as time expands and grows and the true awareness of His energy and His light is developed within humankind.

Reply: Where did He emanate from then, if it wasn't from the God force?

M: It was from the God force, but He was the energy of Love formed into flesh.

Reply: So there is, as it were, from the God force, through Love, a counterbalance to man's destructive free will.

M: Indeed so.

And now, my children, the inevitable, the end of this particular session. Do continue as before, do think about what has taken place this day. Write your questions fairly soon after you have 'chewed it over', shall we say, and formed your understanding. Sometimes with the passage of time, even a few weeks, a salient point might be missed which might make all the difference to the way you ask the question, and thereby the way that we reply to it; but we always enjoy very much being here, speaking with you, loving you, and until the next time we meet, shalom!

Chapter 5

Talk Five, March

The creative force behind God. Crystals, soul and creation. The power and energy of crystals. The breath of God and crystalline structure. Liquid crystal and the body. Prayer.

Master: Beloveds, shalom! This is indeed the way that we enjoy being greeted – that beautiful silence, then a meditation and then the AUMs. It is always, we feel, a fitting beginning to that which spirit will teach. Before we begin, however, we are very aware these days of all the technicalities that have to take place in order that books can be written, transcripts can also be written, and it is almost built-in with us now to check that all is well. So, my son, we ask, are we indeed 'on the air?' (*Chair: You are!*) No doubt one day there will be a different form of recording, one where everyone can relax and not have to switch anything on in order to be recorded – we are speaking, of course, of crystal energy.

Now you might very well ask how crystal energy and the soul can be spoken about in the same talk. Very easily indeed – the soul and crystals are virtually one. This is because at the beginning of time when the God force first was considering allowing His wonderful energy to encompass the entire universe, He indeed formed that crystal energy. He is deep within it, indivisible from it. We wish in a way that we could find a term that would be as familiar as that of the God force, so that when people read our words or listen to them they do not mistake God the Father, that which is the energy that mankind prays to, that people consider to be part of themselves and their lives with the creative God energy – because as we said to you earlier, the creative God energy is very different from all of that which develops from it. Has anyone any ideas as to a good term for this creating energy that could indeed be referred to both in the book and by ourselves in the future? If so, do speak up.

Reply: Could it not be called the life force?

M: It could; anyone else with any ideas?

Reply: The creative life force?

M: We have, of course, referred to it in this way quite often.

Reply: I was thinking of the firmament.

M: Indeed, of course in the Holy Book there is the statement that God created the firmament, which of course implies that the firmament and God are not quite the same entity. Anyone with their original beliefs or anyone grown up with some of the yoga teachings, or anything of that kind? If you think of something during our time together, do give voice to it.

Reply: The collective force?

M: That again is another possibility, because we feel it is time that some of these anomalies are indeed sorted out. With the teachings that we give we try to be as explicit as possible. A lot of the doctrines have their own way of describing God, but to us it is always too full of humanity, too much the echo of man himself. Whereas that can be applicable to the God of prayer, even though it is not strictly accurate, in no way is it applicable to that life energy which began the creation within the universes. This particular energy is of a crystalline structure, therefore absolutely everything within the universe has the same structure within it, modulated very often into what is necessary for the particular planetary energy that was being created, for its reason for the creation, for the reason that it is going to work in harmony with all other planetary and life forces. So it is always important that it is recognised that those parts of everything which relate together must have the same life force within them. If the very first energy that swept through the universe was crystalline, then everything else repeats in that manner. And when you have a large, sweeping statement like that, immediately there is a great deal of thought as to all the different things that you have learnt about that are indeed of that structure.

So when we speak of energy, the kind of energy that is used within such a place as you are now seated, that also is of a crystalline structure which is still developing, still becoming more and more manifest in life as it progresses. So it is safe to say that in a generation or two to come, man can forget about all the electricity generators, all the wires, all the plugs, all the switches, instead he can visualise everything that he needs coming through that integral structure that he can use.

But what of man himself? What part of man contains this structure and why is it that apparently people like those in the medical profession are unaware of it? Science speaks very little about this structure and when it does it is rather more in relation to particles than it is to a human being in relationship to his Earth, yet if the Earth itself is largely comprised of crystals then man obviously must be, because everything within man relates to his Earth. There is a different structure within the planetary elements, but that which relies upon the energy of the planets for support also has within it the same elements that comprise the planets.

We are in a way coming to that point where many people are discussing among themselves life upon the planets and those misguided people who feel that mankind one day will be elevated to the planetary life where they will be able to live, have their children and in hundreds of years hence to form colonies, then Earth can just quietly disintegrate and nobody need worry about what has taken place upon and within it, are daydreaming my children. It is a daydream of those who have watched too many of the planetary programmes that you can now see. All of it is not wrong. Quite a lot of what you might see within those pictures is very possible for the future and after all, what is the future if it is not man's imagination of the moment expressing itself in fact? Without man's ability to imagine life for himself which is better, easier, freer, with fewer burdens, that would never come about. The present society would not be if those in the past hadn't visualised a much better, more wholesome, freer life than they themselves were living, and imagination is a linking with a force outside of man that is able to form a firm structure that man himself can begin to design.

The gradual dawning of knowledge

All of these points we have touched upon in the past. None of this subject is completely new, but if at first when we began to teach we had tried to lay everything out as a fact and as something to be learnt, there would have been many, many people who would have given up. It is only with the gradual dawning of knowledge, the taking in of what has been taught, that those of you now present can understand what we are teaching.

And so this crystal energy that has such importance within us – what part of us? Is it within the skeleton, the blood supply, the cells of the body? How can we relate to it? If we cut ourselves, are we cutting through a structure that can be destroyed in its beauty? Is the whole of the body one magnificent structure like one of these crystals that are within this place, beaming their energy and beaming their light? No, it does not manifest in that way. A crystalline energy is that which is imbued through the breathing, through the thought processes, through the ability of man to relate to the ephemeral. In that way it is within him. There are certain structures that bear a resemblance to crystal. Blood, when it becomes very dried and is no longer fluid enough to be able to work through the veins, through the body, crumbles and under a microscope you would then see tiny, very tiny, crystal particles that form that blood. They can only be seen through a microscope but they are there and yes, that is part of the crystal within your body that is also within the Earth's crust; but we are not thinking of that very matter-of fact, day-to-day form of crystal, we are thinking of the living energy which pulsates from a crystal such as these – something that you can feel when you approach it.

Crystal energy
How can this affect the soul force within its own magnetic field? It is because that which is within those crystals, giving crystals their ability to heal, to transfer healing as well as being within it, transferring it, is also able to draw energies of light, energies of healing into its own structure. Man can do this, it is something man does without even thinking about it, suddenly realising that those who are ill are drawing comfort from a presence, from a touch, even from a thought; and you put a crystal near to them and it doesn't detract from what as a human being you are doing, it adds to it, multiplies it and every time a crystal does this, it does it through the life force of the person who is using the crystal as a transference point.

So there has to be something within that solid state of crystal that relates to man, because man can only relate to that which contains the same particles as he himself has within his life force. So if in your mind you have a visualisation of this God energy, this life force, the original crystalline energy vibrating into space and things forming from it, until you come right down to mankind and you surround man with the solid crystal form and see all of this vibrating with light – and remember your equation: light is energy, is healing, is life. All of these are so important to really understand, not to feel later on it was interesting, difficult to believe but if it is true, why don't the professors with all their knowledge come right out and agree with this? Why haven't they produced this paper on crystal energy for us all to learn? They could have done, a very long time ago. Many of the greatest scientific minds have all the evidence they want in front of them, but they don't want to look foolish, they don't want to have to admit that life is so simple that without all their equations, pages and pages of plus and minuses, that it comes down to that one solid fact – man is crystal, crystal is life, therefore man is also life.

And what of the soul? Of course the soul relates to all of this. There is the soul, one of the first wonderful emissions from that creative force into which everything else that was created is merged. As the soul begins its travelling throughout life, throughout the millions of years that it has taken to get to this point, it carries with it all of this crystal energy and in everything that it touches, like a breath of wind, a breath of air within us, there is that energy proving existence, proving that man cannot live anywhere else except a place that he can relate to, that he is part of. You can almost imagine, can you not, an Earth that is just beginning to emerge from the very primitive state of creation. As the oceans, brimming with crystal energy, gradually begin to diminish, allowing the Earth to rise from its depths, there is man, just beneath the surface, waiting to arise and to greet the sunrise.

The simplicity of God
Life is simple, my children. God is extremely simple to understand. It is mankind that makes Him so complicated, so difficult for everyone to accept. For God, in whatever form, is deep within man, indivisible from man. To say, 'I don't believe in any aspect that God has created,' is simply ignorance being expressed. There are certain things which take place in the cycle of life, in birth and death, which no one should refute, but many people do. If they could absorb those few facts, they would cease to feel so concerned and worried about mankind, his Earth and whether there will be a time when it will cease to exist. Nothing dies, nothing is capable of destruction and death, it is only transmutation from any source that can indeed take place. This was the whole reason why Yeshua came to the Earth, to teach that simple fact. Death is transmuted into life of a different vibration and that vibration continues to develop

throughout all those spheres that we have talked to you about, becoming greater, more illumined as it reaches once more its founder, its Creator – God.

So let us forget just for once all the complications that man himself has made for himself. For a moment visualise within you that God force, think upon it as a nice, neat little vibratory crystal, maybe one like you have yourself for your health or your well-being. See it vibrating deep within your centre, around the area of the solar plexus where there is such sensitivity. See yourself responding to this crystal as it moves throughout your body, emerges into your aura and vibrates and vibrates as it moves away from you into eternity with nothing in its way, nothing that can stop it. There is nothing that is so solid that the crystal energy, as it draws in more and more light, more and more life, as it comes across all the other crystal energy that is within everything in the universe and gathers momentum, cannot enter. The only solid thing that is truly there is your belief or your disbelief in the incarnation of man in the image of God, the image of that wonderful crystal light that was always there, but it was not always manifest in such a luminous and wonderful way. That had to grow, and as it grew it had to take on form, because without form it could not be seen.

As you contemplate the process of the growth of soul, never leave out that vibrant crystal structure within it, because if you do you are making a mockery of everything else that you have learnt throughout the years and making a mockery of what you yourself have developed into through a million or more years of progress.

We will allow our child [*the channel*] to be seated and we will then receive your questions for whatever length of time our son here has laid aside for us to discuss things with you. Thank you for listening to us, my children.

Q: Master, the word that came to mind when you were talking about life force in terms of the yogic philosophies is prana, the life force. (**M:** That is indeed so) *It conjured up an image to me of the breath of God. I thought about this and wondered whether there was a model for the whole of creation, from the emanation of God as a vibratory energy which could be split into several frequency bands which in fact would be defined as the rays, the streams of light from God. It also put me in mind of the fact that the walls of the cells in the human body are liquid crystal. This is* *actually known to science and it struck me that what happens is that we all resonate to a certain frequency within this emanation, this vibratory energy from God. That's how we animate our souls, our bodies and our connection with the Earth. I don't know whether you'd like to make a comment on that?*

M: We were listening with great interest and following through the thought processes and exactly how this formation has come about. The way that you have outlined it is indeed very accurate. We actually were not aware that science has at last reached that conclusion regarding the liquid crystal. Is that a fairly modern theory, or has it been around for some time?

Reply: It's been something which has been discovered by various scientists since about the 1960's. I think what happens in science is that there is very much a compartmentalisation of knowledge, so one speciality might not necessarily know what another speciality discovers, and therefore what you have are various people making theories about the nature of the body in medical science and so on, not actually being aware that a scientist in crystal sciences has discovered that the chemicals within the walls of the cells are in fact liquid crystals and it's just beginning to be put together now. I think this information is coming together because information technology is allowing people now to see a much greater spread of knowledge than the narrow specialisation. So it is becoming accepted fact now.

M: Then maybe someone can write a paper that will go one step further with this vibratory message for the way that the cells are able to adjust to everything in life, outside of the physical form, which is of great importance, and why it is that a simple piece of glass is able to make such a difference to someone who is ill, and why it is that certain crystals have a greater energy force in different people than others. One of the very difficult problems that Elijah has had [*in dictating 'The Way of Stones,' a book on crystal healing*], is trying to equate healing energy into certain crystals for illnesses, and disregard the great changes that come about in the energy of different people when crystals are placed near their bodies. One frequency, as you yourself have just mentioned, can indeed work through a particular class of crystals and be a great advantage to somebody with say polio, or multiple sclerosis, and yet that same group of crystals, if applied to another person with the same illnesses, would have virtually no effect. When we ourselves are speaking to individuals, we can then correlate certain crystals to that person for their own benefit, but when speaking in general it is rather like trying to make one garment fit all people, whether they are large or whether they are very small – it simply cannot be done. So it is important to recognise that this crystal structure varies a very great deal according to the vibration that humanity has developed within themselves, either through mind knowledge, the ability to learn, or through the many, many lives that the aspects have lived, which have increased the Higher Self's ability to understand its own pathway, its own purpose, because all of this does come into that structure – it cannot be set aside from it.

We wish next time to speak rather more on the Higher Self's collective purpose in order to complete this series of talks, because although we have touched upon that purpose from time to time, we haven't given you a visual picture that you can relate to, and it does take in all of the different facets of which we have spoken. It is not just one that is apposite to what you are learning, it is all of these factors, and of course if you had only one aspect interested in coming to the Earth in all this long, long time, then that Higher Self would be very low down in its ability to relate to others and to show a distinct ability to shape the future of the universe, because this is the ultimate need of the Higher Self in its collective state – to be able to improve what the universe set out to achieve; but as we say, this is for the next time, in order to wind up this series and possibly to set people on to a pathway of the realisation of their purpose, and why each individual is so important. Even if they have no religious or spiritual beliefs, they still slot into that vast jigsaw puzzle of the reason humanity was created.

Has anyone else either an opinion or a conclusion that they would like to share with us?

Q: Yes, Master, can I just query what my learned friend here has shared with us about the prana, the breath of life, because I wonder whether that is the same as the creative energy or the creative principle? It seems to me that if one looks at one's own process of creating anything, the very thought process that actually creates something – is that necessarily exactly the same as, say, that which gives the energy for some creation to actually take place?

M: No, not absolutely, it isn't, but man will never really catch up with creation's vision of the future, because that vision was for things to progress – never to stand still, always to move forward, to multiply, to become greater, both in numbers and in the visualisation of what lies ahead. This is why man has been given a brain, why he is able through the collective mind to visualise that which has not yet occurred within his part of the world, or within his own life span. Everything is constantly moving within that vibration, within that flux. There has to be an allowance for what has not occurred before, but prana is an excellent way for most people to consider that breath to be. Although of course where man is concerned his prana is spasmodic, it comes and goes according to his energy, according to his own ability to expand and grow, whereas the prana, shall we say, of the God force never diminishes, it is always expanding, and within that expansion man takes his primary role. He is able to relax, be part of this, to know he is supported and man is, after all, only a carbon copy of what God's vision of humanity originally was and God Itself is still in that creative process of making His vision better and stronger and more beautiful.

Reply: *In the yogic tradition this force is seen in three ways – as the creative force, the sustaining force and also the destructive force – that which allows it to return. Would you consider that this is all prana* in terms of the God force?*

M: Not the destructive element. There is nothing within the God prana, shall we say, which induces or allows destruction.

Reply: *Perhaps I should have said transmuting, rather than destruction.*

M: That would have been a better word, because there is the positive and negative in absolutely everything, but the negative isn't always destructive, as you will agree. Where destruction comes about, it is man's inability for perfection. He is always striving for it, but always just falling short of that ability to create something that is more beautiful, more permanent than

---

*Later research indicated that in Yogic terminology Purusha is the creative mind which combines with Prkriti to create matter. This was put to the Master who commented, 'That sounds much better because really nothing is destroyed, nothing disappears, it is purely and simply a transformation.'

what has been created before; but within the God energy that never occurs because it is impossible for that energy ever to become transmuted within itself. It is only man's energy which is transmuted, not the God force.

Reply: If I may just come back very quickly, how then can man's energy be outside that of the energy which created man in the first place?

M: Because of man's inability to recognise the God force within himself. He always visualises himself as outside of it. God is something 'out there;' God is something you move toward, you pray to. If man could realise that he is praying to his own centre, to that which vibrates within himself, instead of the 'Please may I have?' or 'Please don't take this away from me,' if there were an affirmation along the lines of, 'May the God within bring to me that which I need, that which is right for me,' then everything that supports man, be it his work, his health, the love he draws to himself, the love that he distributes to others, would be there in the right quantity, in the right ability for it to take place. It is the God within which is what man is constantly seeking and falling short of, because of doubt, because of fear.

Q: Could you say how much crystal exists within the Earth?

M: That is difficult because it does vary in different areas of the world. It is not consistent. It is like so many things which exist in the Earth itself – some parts of the country will be richer in a phosphate than others, others find that the actual Earth itself in which people plant things varies in its composition. You can have rich green vegetables in one area, in another you can have wonderful fruit trees abundant in their fruits, so it is not evenly distributed. We suppose that if you take the whole Earth as a unit, it would be something like 25%, give or take a little.

Reply: Mostly at the core of the Earth, being distributed upwards?

M: Yes, the core itself is totally of a crystal structure and the energy from it is distributed, layer upon layer, strata upon strata, until there are particles in varying strength near the surface of the Earth.

Reply: *Do any of the other planets share a crystal centre?*

M: They all have a crystal centre but different energies are distributed within the different planets. Earth, of course, we recognise as a planet and it has a different crystal energy than that of any of the other planets.

Reply: *So what prevents man from colonising the planets is not necessarily technology, but more an acceptance of a different force?*

M: To start with, the crystal energy within man, as we implied earlier, relates to his Earth. It does not relate to the medium of crystal energy which is within the planets. There are one or two which are fairly similar, even if you ignore the fact of the lack of oxygen and the lack of temperature that man can relate to, even if all those things were altered to accept man's life upon them, it would be a different energy force from their crystal structure than man has within his Earth.

Now there is a very interesting hypothesis here – inasmuch as if man could start a colony – if there were sufficient components that could travel with him in his spacecraft to form a habitat for him, then maybe future generations that are born upon that planet might well begin to absorb the energy field from that planet, they might give rise to a species that could live upon it without having to rely all the time on the same energies as Earth. That is not outside the realm of reason, but it would take a very long time before it happened and there would be a great number of deaths before a way was found to create that particular life, of course he wouldn't look exactly like man looks – he couldn't. He wouldn't have lungs, he wouldn't breathe so he wouldn't need to have things like a nose to breathe through. We don't need to go further, you know what we mean here.

Q: *Master, you mentioned two forms of crystal, which are liquid and solid. I have only seen the solid form and since you spoke of crystal energy, does that mean that it's got many other forms than solid and liquid and does it mean that the whole universe is crystal, or the whole energy has got a huge element of crystal in it?*

M: That is so – it's virtually in everything, but if you are looking simply upon an energy, if you look at your own body, something makes it move, does it not? Something allows that movement within your body to take place, you might say, 'Yes, the response within my brain which relates to whether I move my hand or my arm or my leg.' Of course that is so, but there is also an energy field within humanity without which there would be no thought, there would be no movement, there would be no ability for anything at all to take place. There would be total inertia and that energy field is also of a crystal structure. It is invisible but it is there and all those who live upon the Earth and have their movement, they recognise it as a kinetic energy. It is one of force and if something is of force then it has to have a motivation behind that force, which is God. It gets more complicated, does it not? There doesn't seem to be a real way of simplifying any of this.

Reply: So you would call it kinetic force?

M: That would be our term for it, yes.

Q: We've talked about how the different light streams* denote different purposes and I was wondering if the different crystals relate to different purposes and different light streams and if they do, is it as straightforward as rose quartz for people on the pink stream, or green crystals relating to the green stream and can those crystals help us to recognise and achieve our purpose?

M: It can indeed be applied in that over-simplified way for those who feel they want to begin to use crystals for health and well-being, or for strengthening themselves or protecting themselves, if they are aware of the light stream that predominates within their aspect, then yes, they can use those particular crystals but they would need to programme them. This is something that must never be overlooked – that any crystal, however simple or complicated it may be, should not be used for a specific purpose unless it has been (a) divined for that purpose and (b) prepared for that use. It goes without saying that it should

---

*To the Master, light and colour are not just visual; they are imbued with both meaning and purpose. Light streams are how the Higher Self organises the learning pattern for the incarnating soul and they span the entire spectrum of colour. For example, someone incarnating within the pink light stream will have that colour strongly within their aura; also they will probably choose work and life experiences that help them learn about and express the compassion and humanity that characterises this light stream. See Appendix A.

also be cleansed, so that any energy that might have remained within it or upon it from another outside force can be removed. So if all of this is taken into account and you decide that with a pink stream you will use a rose quartz, then you must pro-gramme that crystal for the best possible energy within your own energy. So it cannot be done – and this is the important point – it cannot be done by another person on your behalf, we have heard that quite a lot of people say, 'I am going to give a certain crystal to my patient and I have programmed that crystal to help him or her with their illness.' That should never be done. They can tell the patient what to do, which is very simple – having cleansed it, they hold it to their forehead, because the strongest ray of energy for a crystal comes forth from that area of the body, and simply either manufacture a thought for the crystal as to what it will be doing, or it can be spoken by the voice as to what it wishes the crystal to do. Then that crystal will be definitely for the person to whom it has been given, or who has chosen it.

So this is one of the lessons regarding crystals that all of you can take on board for the future. Give somebody else a crystal by all means, but remind them not to use it until those particular criteria have been followed. Later on, with more knowledge of the different crystals and their functions, people can go forward and have a wonderful variety of different kinds of crystal for different purposes, but a very good way to start is to find out what your particular colour stream may be. It is not everyone who is able to tell this to another person, or for the individual to know themselves.

Reply: *But it is colour co-ordinated. For example, if you are of the blue stream you use a blue crystal, if you are from the green stream then a green crystal, and so on?*

M: You don't necessarily have to, but as we say, you can. It's a good place to start. As long as you feel the vibration of a crystal and it seems to relate to you, if you see one and you are drawn to it, that crystal does something to you, you can't turn away from it, you've got to have it. Or you feel it is exactly right for your child or your partner or your friend, then it is literally calling to you and you are listening to that silent little voice within it and obeying it.

Reply: *But it could be calling to you for an eye complaint, or a skin disorder, and not anything to do with your light stream?*

M: Of course it could, and there again a little bit of knowledge is needed somewhere, in order to divine its purpose. We usually suggest that a pendulum is the best way, although some people can do it simply by relating to the crystal and talking to it and getting to their own satisfaction an answer back; or they can use the palm of their hand by placing it over the crystal and asking the crystal questions. There will be a vibratory force which will be the yes or no that relates to the individual.

Q: *Referring back to prayer which you spoke of earlier, as the majority of people do pray to an external God force and they don't perceive it as part of themselves, what effect does that have, if any?*

M: Oh, it can only have a good effect. Nothing is decried in any way. If there is a prayer from the heart, particularly because of sadness or sorrow, or a need for God to relate to the person, that prayer is never unheeded. The fact that most of humanity think that they are praying to an external force, maybe even have a visualisation of what it may be, does not stop the prayer reaching its source, but it is usually man himself who makes that prayer come alive, makes it reality, actually allows it to take place. You could say that by emitting a prayer you are giving yourself an incentive to overcome the adverse situation or the pain or the fear, whatever it may be. You are stimulating yourself into action – you think that you are demanding something or pleading for something, but it is the reaction of the self that makes it a reality. Does this make sense to you all? (*All: Yes*) No one really can say to God, 'Take away this agony, take away this pain,' without there being an inner response which might say, 'I must make an effort myself, I've got to find a way that this can indeed be overcome,' and this is the main joy of prayer – a conversation with the God force within.

(*To the Chair*) A talk one day on prayer would be good, my son. Not a series, just a talk!

Q: *I wanted to go back – the image that I had in my mind when you talked about creation was of crystals or crystalline structure being the nervous system of creation. Is that a fair interpretation of what you meant?*

M: Very well put, yes. There are, as you gather, quite a few ways of describing it because it is so versatile, because it relates to so many different aspects of creation that there can be many ways of visualising it or of describing it, but yes, that would be one of them. Can we ask the speaker who was talking about the liquid crystal of cells, has anything yet been discovered or proved regarding the sheath lining of the nervous system?

Reply: Not as far as I know, Master. I have only recently learned of the walls of the cells being of the nature of a liquid crystal. I imagine that most of the cell walls in the body would have this same chemical structure. In other words, it would be consistent throughout the human body so that the whole structure hung together, and there must also therefore be some kind of communication between the cells of the body in order for us to have the intelligent structure that we do actually manifest as a human body.

M: That is so and, of course, all the sheath lining of the nervous structure has a very strong crystal representation, so it might be nice to set the ball rolling amongst a few sceptics to see with their research whether they can ultimately agree with this.

Reply: Well, as you know I am compiling your book, 'The Way of Truth,' and I was going to put in a section about the liquid crystal nature of the cell walls. I think it also explains in a very graphic way the meditation on the single cell [a healing meditation which focusses attention on a single cell, see Appendix B], *because there in fact you are visualising the whole structure with that crystal nature.*

M: Indeed so, and it would be rather good if everybody read that particular transcript, because it would help all the healers, whether they use crystals or whether they are using the Christos energy, to understand the single cell principle of healing. So we really would recommend that particular one.

Q: What about the geometric structure of the crystals – is there a specific geometric structure or is this variable?

M: They are variable, and if you are also referring to the designs they are fashioned into, that makes absolutely no difference. You can have a very large, quite ornate crystal which is beautiful to look at, but it can be relatively low in energy and you can have another crystal that absolutely vibrates with light but is very small that has a wonderful healing capacity. We are not decrying the one that is lower in energy, it can be used for a different purpose, but it wouldn't have the same ability to transform within a person, to make them well, as maybe that very small, versatile crystal could do.

Reply: I was thinking of it more on a cellular level.

M: Yes, we realise that, and of course different crystals do have a different cellular vibration and can work on those levels in healing. We hope that in the future they will be used more and more in operating theatres instead of the scalpels and knives and other impedimenta which simply cut through the structure, but will work in a natural way with it, to harmonise the body and gradually deter different organs from being cut out and replaced, but healed internally with different crystals. All of this will indeed come about as people accept more the purpose of crystals and the true strength and energy that is within them.

Q: Master, you said that souls had a crystal structure. Is it then that all souls have a basic crystal structure which is the same throughout, or do souls have different crystal structures?

M: They have a basic structure, in the same way as all humans have the same organs within their body, they are all virtually the same to look at, but they have different personalities, different shapes and sizes and colours and so forth. So the soul is the same, it has its crystal structure but according to the development through the Higher Self as it is finding more and more its purpose in fulfilling it, so that structure also changes. We think that we should now leave the discussion at the point we have reached, maybe for you to ponder upon. There might be a question or two that will arise in our next talk with you, which is our last one. We do intend to make that as much as possible a winding up of what we have been sharing with you, but the majority of the time is to be for your questions. So if you also can go over in your minds the main contents of these different talks and anything that you think could be clarified or added to, to come along with those questions, which will make a grand finale for this series, will it not? We really are delighted to know that so many of you have this interest in these series, and we know that our son hopes in the future to continue with different subject matters, and to see the radiance of you all before us will indeed be a delight.

So just for a moment, my children, link your hands with each row, not of course to link with the row behind, just the row that you are in. Now, tune in to the crystalline structure of the person next to you. See what kind of response you get within your mind, see whether you can work out the colour stream of the person, see whether you can feel that that structure is in harmony with your own, whether there is a reason for you relating to the person, or feeling you want to stand apart from them. We are not going to ask your reactions, we simply want you to feel the reaction and think about it until next time, because it might very well give you an inner link with personality, with soul structure, that can help your quest for knowledge.

While you are linked in this way, perhaps our son can do whatever conclusion he wishes, so that we can move away from our child and allow her to join in the ending. Shalom.

Chapter 6

Talk Six, April

The Higher Self or Oversoul, its learning and purpose. A web of relationship. The life of the Arimathean. Reincarnation and death. Movement beyond the spheres of light. The way of soul.

Master: Welcome my children. Shalom! When we were considering the subject matter for the last occasion of the soul, we had virtually decided that as so much had been given, thought upon and questioned, that to give the whole of the session to further questions might be a good idea; but those who are within my own Higher Self as Joseph of Arimathea and whose collective consciousness has been assisting with the subjects and with the co-ordination of them, thought it might be a good idea if they were mentioned, at least in passing, as to how their collective memory had come into being, after being individual aspects in the same way as yourselves and I myself have been two thousand years ago. Certainly it is good to be practical on occasions, as it is that practicality that gives more evidence, 'drives home,' as it were, the meaning of aspects of the soul and what truly occurs further along the line, once they have no longer to come to the Earth and to find a life that will give even greater purpose to the whole lesson.

An overall lesson
You have learnt that each Higher Self or Oversoul has a particular overall lesson to which all the aspects contribute, but what of those who have either elected not to come to the Earth, or who have been dissuaded from so doing? It is never easy to visualise something that has never been seen or felt or heard, so we realise how very difficult it has been for all of those following the soul learnings and teachings to understand truly what an aspect represents. We have tried to help you visualise the entire soul as being akin to the body, the aspects akin to the cells that form the body, and this is as close as we can achieve for a visual understanding of an Oversoul. The beautiful light that shines within an Oversoul is like a reflection of all the many colours and the energy patterns which evoke those colours reflecting on each of the cells or aspects within it. It is more difficult to realise that each one is individual to the others; but again, if you think of humanity within the world and how

everyone who lives is just that little bit different from fellow man in features, in height, in build, so many permutations – what really sets individuals apart, one from another? How can we differentiate between identical twins for example if they look so absolutely alike? Of course, it is the personality, it is that little bit extra, that little flavour of non-uniformity which helps us to know them apart. Again the principle is much the same when it comes to the Oversoul. We see it as a reflection of meticulous energies reflected in colour and you would hardly conceive the idea that with so many billions of total souls, of Higher Selves, of Oversouls, that each one would have a slightly different energy pattern from the others, but it is so. Each of these energy patterns is reflected in each single aspect. This is what gives the aspect its unique status, why whichever one might be chosen to continue that pathway can do so, aware of all that has gone before.

Those among you who are aware of patterns of electricity, for example, people who work on component parts for differ-ent vehicles or machines, they know there must be a unit to which everything else conforms and reflects. It is exactly the same when it comes to living and to the soul reflecting within the personality. For simplicity you could say that each aspect reflects its own personality which it imbibes into the embryo and then into the human being that results from that concep-tion. Forget for a moment the human status, the DNA, the life reflected through the centuries, mingling and intermingling with other members of the family; it is all important, it is all part of the Divine Plan, but that is the human side which is not reflected within the Higher Self. So having decided that twenty or thirty aspects have come into life and are living in various parts of the world, possibly never to meet, what could possibly be the reason that they would all elect to come? What is that unified purpose, and exactly how much jurisdiction does the Oversoul place on which aspect goes where, when and why?

Purpose and the Higher Self
Any energy pattern that is working for a purpose has to be very versatile. You cannot have a national grid that will supply warmth and light to every home within its radius without being aware of the intricacy of the pattern which provides it. Apply exactly the same principle within the Higher Self and its aspects and you will realise that as each aspect is born within its chosen

vehicle there is an interlinking of purpose. If you have an aspect in Australia and you never travel there and he never travels to where you are, there is still that same purpose that is guiding his life as guides yours. So how do you relate? Is it a case of going toward the Higher Self every time and consciously speaking with it, receiving directions from it, or is there a simpler way? That simpler way is indeed the mind. When we have spoken of the veil of thought which is indeed part of the Universal Mind, it is a pattern that everyone automatically reaches toward in order to be able to relate to mankind in general. Your thought pattern is part of the pattern of everyone else that lives. There is also part of that pattern that relates to everyone that has passed into spirit. If it were not so, how could those among you that are present now realise there are times when you link with ourselves, either consciously through request, or when we link with you to give you strength, to help you to cope with whatever situation you are experiencing at that time? So, of course, it is an interlinking pattern which encompasses everything that has lived and everything that will live.

A mental web

We often use the term 'a web,' very much like the beautiful web that spiders weave. Have you ever really looked at them, have you ever watched that spider commence the web, drawing from its body that ultra-fine single thread that commences the weaving? Have you ever seen a female spider give birth in the centre of that web? Another time do not break the thread, do not with disgust banish it from your home as being unclean, but watch, see that which takes place. It is a matter only of hours and that beautiful web is there, providing everything that the female and its child might want. The web is very similar to that which exudes from the Oversoul and that also relates very much to the much greater soul which is attributed to the Creative Force. So you imagine that this God-essence is in the centre of this vast web and that everything it gives birth to has its own place within it; and does it not also represent that spiral that we so often mention? There in the centre is the spiral as it has been reached at this moment in time, on the verge of the New Age, the verge of another opportunity for man. The outer perimeter is that which occurred two thousand years ago and drew into itself the beginnings of new opportunity, new life for man to weave within himself.

Very gradually the picture of the Oversoul begins to take shape, but it is still difficult to conceive as to why it should need to. Why should God the Creator conceive of such an intricate idea as to people the world with this mind-link when they do not know and often do not care about each other? That link is the desire of the Oversoul to experience certain patterns of living at different times within the universe, which is why all those now living upon the Earth are experiencing time as it is relevant to this moment. So your other aspect, although it has no understanding of your existence, your life, has chosen when to come and where, to experience another side of what you are experiencing in your life now and this is what has occurred throughout the life of my own Higher Self.

The life of Joseph of Arimathea
Since the beginning of man's emergence into the Earth world, so aspects have become born to experience; just as yours have and you had an equal opportunity, as did I, to form links through the mind and through prayer with both God and with that of myself that had gone before. Some have the desire to do this more strongly than others. As Joseph I was one of those that had an intense, burning desire to be aware of the past and how it linked with my own life at that time, why it was that I should have been born, formed the earthly links that I did, why I was going through that pattern of existence, much of it very sad, very traumatic, why I had not chosen a very different life, more peaceful, placid, with less danger. [*See biography, 'The Way of Love,' compiled by Peter Wheeler.*]

So why have you chosen the origins that you have within yourselves? Some of you were born in other countries; why did you come here, why are you now seated together and we are speaking with you? Because that 'we' is very much individual selves, now assured of their purpose and realising as they hold on to the fragile links of the web that their source of succour, of knowledge, was universal and identical, one to the other. As you perceive your Higher Self you realise that you too are a very important part of all the living and learning that the other selves, or aspects, have already enjoyed. Your knowledge is in part their knowledge and your future is in part their future. They are aware of it through your consciousness and you are aware of their experience through your subconscious.

So what is the link between the consciousness of now and

the subconscious which reflects everything that your Oversoul has experienced? The link is God, the link is the mastermind behind all existence, the large spider in the centre of that web from which all life flows. So no one, whatever their beliefs or non-beliefs may be, can escape from Truth. There is but one Truth and it exists, even if there are different ways of portraying it, even if there are those who are adamant in their disbelief of life after death, of a Creator, of a unified purpose, or of any kind of unification that links man, one with another. There is no other explanation how scientists with a straight face can possibly say that man is not linked in any way except through his DNA to the parents and grandparents and so forth, of the past. We will never understand this. In so many ways they have great knowledge, they have minds that can dissect, multiply and divide to a very great degree, but that very simple equation, that of the source emanating from God, seems to elude them.

The source of truth
What is in a name? A name has no true purpose except to identify something that otherwise would be difficult to relate to. We don't mind what name you might give that source of energy, of life, anything that pleases you. We do not mind whether you think of that which has been teaching you all these months as a single entity or as one that is part of a much greater whole. The fact remains that the source of Truth is shared amongst all that link with you and help your growth. It is an indisputable fact of the linking with the other Teachers of Light that have come to speak, not within the same unified Higher Self, but because of linking throughout different lives, to learn something more that can be shared, stored and then given to such as yourselves when that time is right. It is not by chance that those Teachers have the same vision but project it in different ways, nor yet that there is indeed a hierarchy which has come through the development of understanding and knowledge. There must always be those that have a little more knowledge, a little more understanding to share with those that seek. If everyone was on the same standard of knowledge as each other it would be a very dull world indeed, with very little in the way of variety of talents and understandings to share.

So the soul must go through all this very varied view on life to achieve what? To achieve at some time 'returning to base' as it were, the stored-up knowledge of all those lives? Is it to be put into a safe and the door locked to fester there, or does it continue to be shared and to grow? The short answer is yes, it does, it continues to expand and grow. There is no limit placed on what you learn or how you learn it. If you touch the Earth for a few minutes and return to spirit, it makes its mark upon humanity and the growth of humanity because all of that knowledge is shared amongst the individual Oversouls and it also expands toward the God force, keeping it vibrating, keeping the motion of the universe continuous as it expands and grows. It is all turned into energy, every thought, every action, every motive, even that which you desire to do and never have still has its place within the thought pattern in the universe. Nothing is wasted. There have been times on occasions we have reiterated the words 'there is no death.' That is because everything is transmuted into another form of life. Nothing is wasted.

The pattern of the soul as it moves through time has its own reason for that expansion, and therefore as your souls link together with the united purpose of spiritual growth you add 'flavour,' as it were, to that knowledge as a group, very much as you do as individual people linking and forming that group. Each time you speak to another and you reflect the knowledge that you have imbibed there is yet another link within the endless chain of awareness that flowed billions of years ago into the universe and continues to do so until the end of time.

The memory of the soul
To sum up that which we wish to say to you before we ask for your questions, we will say this: you, within yourself, the individual you, your mind, your thought is engineered from a similar pattern to my own. You reach out into that consciousness that began so long ago with the first aspect as it came to Earth and that aspect still has a purpose to unite with you, to give you awareness, to enable you to challenge life at the moment, to be consciously aware when you learn of historical records, to know that they are right or they are wrong. It is as though you had visited every place in every year since that time began and carried the memories forward to this present moment. That is your pathway, that is the Way of Soul and the purpose it was given to create further life, further expression, further knowledge. Your world will never cease to be while the intelligence of man links with his soul and with its Higher Self.

We have very much enjoyed this series and we will look forward collectively as the Higher Self or Overself of Joseph to conducting further series with the other spiritual teachers who have linked with us over the years, but let us now for the remainder of the allotted time speak together to answer those questions that you have brought to ask us.

Q: You have always emphasised how the individual aspects of the Higher Self or Oversoul develop their own personalities, but since there is this linking and sharing, and the knowledge and experience come forward from the aspects of the past to the aspects of the present, doesn't that mean that over time the personalities become similar? Aren't we the sum of all that has gone before?

M: The longer that an aspect remains in spirit, the less that personality is relevant to what is taking place as a whole. There are ays remnants of it, but it is no longer as vivid as it is when it eaking with others, relating to others, expressing that per ty as a living, vibrant being. Of course you are correct ome personalities within the Higher Self are very similar, v if there is a similar purpose to be learnt. Many may use they enjoy the change of energies from one age as indeed is occurring now. Many may come is a particular purpose to be engendered, like the C ht have been coming into the Earth and are co. ┤ to be an overlapping of similar person alities it is to the purpose that that aspect achieve into life that is the really important reasonin f people come and they give up on learning, t. y either haven't sufficient growth within themse. to learn, or maybe they have very little ego, or too mu whatever the case may be, to learn spiritually, then that life is of no true accord and no true reality, so it is not recorded. Within the Akashic we only record those lives which have given a real purpose to living, which have helped even in a limited way for other people to understand their greater purpose, to live with more peace, more vibrancy in their lives. Any other life is laid to one side as a material experience of no true worth. So you might find that through all those hundreds and thousands of lifetimes, only a very small number of these go down in the annals of time as worthy of memory.

Q: Master, you spoke of the aspect returning to the spiritual realms and sharing with the Oversoul its experiences. When the aspect is upon the Earth, is it still possible for it to share the experiences it is going through, and also receive the experiences of other aspects while it is living upon the Earth? In other words, is it a two-way thing while it is still living?

M: Yes indeed, the short answer to that is all these things are possible and do indeed take place, whether it is on a truly conscious level when you are aware of this and have pleasure in recalling it, or whether it is done subliminally to be able to give you encouragement to go forward, especially at a time when all other beliefs or all other actions might not seem to have a purpose. Let us take the people as an example who at this moment are having to flee from their homes, flee from their countries [*Here the Master is referring to the Kosovar refugees.*] Many have asked and some have asked ourselves, 'What can their purpose of living be, to have everything that was safe and comfortable shattered in this way?' Well, it is partly to do with their karma and partly to do with what the inner soul desired for this particular life, to have that experience.

The soul's design and the future
One of the main reasons for not looking into the future, for not being able to plan ahead to any great purpose, is so that the soul's design will have predominance over the personality, but the kind of life you might have presented for yourself can be interwoven with what the soul needs to learn and to project. So although to yourselves it might seem dreadful that they are put through this state of flux and to them also while it is happening, the greater reason for it all is there to reflect upon in the future. Then, when the purpose of that great upheaval is truly understood man himself can either return to build a better country, a better life, or commence a new life in another part of the world that the soul already knew would take place, whether it was from a horrendous happening or alternatively from absolute choice.

If life was just for the quiet, comfortable living nothing would ever have been achieved from the very beginning of the world. Life then was more horrendous, more painful than it is now, because man has moved forward, he has moved on from those very primitive times. Although some things still reflect that primitive aspect, it is still right for what is being achieved now in preparation for the future.

Q: Master, is the fact that the West has intervened in international conflicts by sending in bombers also part of the overall plan? Do you think that the West should interfere in this war?

M: It is difficult to state absolutely regarding this. There are many alternatives as to how in some of these situations intervention can bring violence to an end and enable the purpose of the closing months of the age to be fulfilled. One of them is through the interference of more liberated countries that have learnt themselves from the past how hideous it is to be under domination and how they have fought to ensure that it will never happens again, who feel that their intervention may prevent a more widespread war that would cause even more deaths and destruction if some of the weapons of war were unleashed. There might have been another way, but that seemed to be the logical way to prevent these hideous events escalating and becoming much greater. It is the objectivity that we look at rather than the mode of action which was chosen. To us it is always important to intervene when humankind are at risk. Things, homes, factories are never as important as humankind itself and sometimes it is a choice between several things as to what survives and what is destroyed.

In general the West has gone through most of the processes of war and survived, so it has a greater freedom to make that choice and to use it to ultimately help others. We only hope that such choices bear fruit; although sometime there may be many who will perish. We have to bear in mind the fact that many souls would know it is time to pass that divide and return to spirit. Many others have evoked a karma which necessitates the kind of passing that they are living through, while others, because of the progress of their own Higher Self, their own Oversoul, need to experience it to pass on to others that come as a result of the war, to have a greater sense of the urgency and the need for world peace. As it has been said many times, the means is father to the end.

Q: One thing that has baffled me about studying the soul and the aspects is that in previous disciplines I have always come to believe that there was that which is imperishable within us, that which is eternal and that presumably is the soul. What I can't quite understand is that the aspect is for this life, then the aspect returns to the spiritual realms and is enlightened as to what the life meant. Then you spoke of the aspect fading and yet surely we do not then become extinct. Surely there is that in us which continues to experience and to grow, to eventually join with the Higher Self and then with the Creative Logos? It is said on this path that we only have one life for each aspect, and yet other paths state that we are continually reincarnated and I find it difficult to bring those two strands together. Can you help me?

M: You misunderstood, we referred to the personality as fading, not the aspect. Have you not been aware of a person whose life has left them, a person maybe that you have loved very greatly, you've loved them very largely because of the personality they have expressed? They are that person, the personality is that person, not because they are a great soul or a lesser soul, or because that soul wishes to learn a particular lesson. You love them because of what they exude as being them, and have you not seen within moments of death that that body which is lying there no longer seems to have that same beauty, that same awareness? It is because the personality has gone with the life force, the personality and that life force which is the breath of God, which links and which enables the human self to be what it is, to learn what it is, to share what it is, that has left that body, which will immediately begin to perish. It is the God spirit, the God force that links all the way through life with the soul aspect that provides the humanness that we value so much in those we love.

Reincarnation
The second part of your question regarding reincarnation – different people have a different understanding of what this action means. Some feel it is the entire soul that comes into life, time after time after time. What we teach is not so very different. That soul, that Overself learns just as much from the individual lives that the aspects portray, probably even more so than if it came into the personality with every life. That would be shedding the personality as another life came into being, it would have to. It would mean that the personality had nowhere to go. That person who remembers you and who you remember, who you talk to in your mind, who you feel is travelling with you to

familiar places, holiday places, other places that you have shared so many memories, where would that personality go if it had nothing to be attached to? It would be as though the Higher Self had hundreds and thousands of different faces, different minds, different understandings and as it came into being it would exude all of these. It cannot be so. So the fact that there are all these aspects that can individually learn, concentrate on that life to a total understanding of it, but still reach up to the Overself with its understanding of what that soul desires to experience and learn from with all these different lives, able also to spread out to the other aspects, to link for a little learning here, a little understanding there, a link with the past for someone that you have met at this moment, it is only possible because it is all broken down into these aspects in order that the soul may learn.

So those that believe in the one soul and the many incarnations are limiting their beliefs, limiting themselves, but those who accept that all these aspects belong within that intricate web, they are expanding their minds, expanding the knowledge that they want to gain from and learn from. So look at it that way, my son and you will have a greater vision, a wider vision of what the Oversoul wishes to provide.

Reply: So can I say then that I am in truth the Oversoul?

M: You are an integral part of the Oversoul with an interchange of the vast knowledge that the Oversoul has from all its many aspects. You are also in touch with all those aspects but you are the individual aspect that is learning from and enjoying this life at this time. It is steps forward, linking all the time. If you were the Oversoul you would not be able to believe in all the other lives having a particular purpose that strengthens, develops, enlarges that Oversoul on its journey, on its pathway to perfection and to join the God force ultimately and rejoice in it.

Reply: So my aspect then will not live again?

M: Indeed not.

Q: After a discussion we once had I calculated that on average it takes two to three hundred thousand incarnations to fulfil one Higher Self. Often those incarnations are very difficult – life has been called a 'vale of tears' – so to return that many times to quite difficult, often very painful learning experiences is quite a commitment. What is the reward at the end of that journey?

M: The reward is to be within that bliss state, the state of utter awareness of the God force which shares within Itself and to all It reflects upon the absolute knowledge of existence. Not having to think, little bit by little bit, what's being experienced, what's being learnt, filling page after page of recollection and trying to understand how that bit of life works with another bit of life, how when you were one year old, how what you knew then can possibly be the same as when you are in your eighties or nineties. It is the at-one-ness of the self, all that knowledge reflected in the absolute awareness that comes at the journey's end, moving into the God force, that creative energy that already had all knowledge of all things and wished the soul to experience the same understanding.

There was no selfishness in that act, in fact there was no pre-conceived idea, 'I will make these people suffer, I will show them what it is like,' nothing of this kind; the loving God force only wanted to share the experience of absolute knowledge, but it couldn't do that with something that had never experienced one decimal point of it – it could not do this. It could only share enlightenment with the enlightened, and when you think that when you speak with a young child who is just beginning to understand life itself, with their endless questions, 'Why is this? Why is that?' which are often so difficult to answer even though you have lived all those years more than the child has, how it makes you think as to whether you really understand the basis of the questions and answers you give.

The lessons of the soul

Imagine a God force who has an absolute understanding trying to relate this to a soul that has learnt virtually nothing. The lifetimes upon the Earth may seem prosaic, they may seem only of the material or the physical, but they also encourage the mind to learn, to accept, to understand, and all the lessons are linked with the mind, they are linked with the soul's understanding and the soul becomes deepened and enriched by the learning that takes place. If it is only to accept and understand a sympathetic reaction, how to overcome prejudice, how to accept the life, the being of another and his or her rights – it can be a very small lesson and another life can have a very great lesson – but it is all these lessons drawn together which form enlightenment. The pathway of soul is to allow that enlightenment ultimately to take place until that absolute knowledge is indeed the bliss state that we are often promised, but equally as often we fail to accept exists.

We have enjoyed today, speaking with you, being aware of your energies as they reach toward us, being aware of what has gone into the preparation of your questions. We sincerely hope that when all of this is dealt with in a practical way and is presented for your further enlightenment and the enlightenment of others who read it, that it will present a picture of that pathway which is truly a way of life, a way of understanding, that the true God force, reflected as soul needs it, as soul desires it, will be fulfilled. We bid you farewell until the next series, my children. Shalom.

Parallel Worlds

*During the course of these talks one of the group members ques-
tioned the Master about parallel worlds in a private session. The
resulting dialogue is included here at the Master's request.*

*Question: I have recently been reading some of what you have said
in the past about parallel worlds. I think I already understand the
basis of what you have said about the spirit worlds being parallel
to the world that in which I exist. They all exist in the same space
but with a separate vibration. If I understand your words, the
world that is parallel to ours, that exists within our time frame is
simply on a slightly different vibration. You said that it is possible
to visit that world, not just for someone like me but you used the
analogy of trauma in the First World War and a soldier suddenly
finding himself in a place of tranquillity prior to coming back to
this world and the horror of that war. When that happens would
you move as a body to that other world and find yourself in that
other world physically or is it just a movement within the mind?*

Master: It is usually an actual movement from one vibration
into another keeping their body, their intellect, their awareness
of everything about them, yet being aware that they are experiencing at a different level of consciousness than that which has
been taking place up to that moment of transition. We can
explain initially, which we may very well have done in what you
have read, that the two vibrational worlds are very much opposite to each other in what they are denoting. If the soul desires
action, learning, true karmic representation within its Higher
Self then it might very well choose incarnation in the world that
is going through a great deal of trauma, such as occurred in the
two major world wars.

Even in this particular world in which you are located and
all your friends, it is to be aware of the fears that are taking place
from time to time though not being embroiled in the actions
whereas the parallel world will be less full of action but has just
as much purpose on a different fundamental understanding.
Soldiers in the battlefield possibly with a great deal of trauma,
both mentally and physically, might well if they continue in that
situation find that they are moving into a death pattern and yet
the soul does not really want that experience; it simply wants

the experience that has been undertaken and it will thereby shift the body, the personality, into another existence or respite. If you are standing on the battlefield with another soldier and suddenly you look round and that soldier is no longer within your view you might think one of two things to yourself – you might think that he had run for cover and you had missed him suddenly moving away or you might think that he had been blown to pieces which might fill you with horror, it might make you yourself take some action which otherwise you would not have contemplated.

Like a dream

Everything that takes place in life from the smallest need to the greatest is as a result either of your thoughts, your actions or the actions of another. Nothing just happens – it always is for a reason. Now what may very well have happened with that soldier is the soul would have been aware that there would indeed at any moment be an explosion or the heart might give out with the sheer fear, the trauma that is taking place. Therefore the whole body and personality are moved vibrationally into a parallel world. That person suddenly being aware of being in exactly the same spot but without any sign of battle, no sign of anything that disturbs the peace, just the countryside, the birds singing and so forth, would immediately think, 'Did I dream what has been taking place or am I dreaming now? Have I fallen asleep with sheer desperate tiredness and this is my dream world?'

Such occasions happened a great deal, but there usually is a great trauma which occurs for the soul to be so specific, so sure, that the action will be life-saving, sanity-saving. The kind of trauma other than that which we have described could well be a very, very serious illness and if death is to be averted then sometimes the traumatic situation takes people out of their senses, allows them to recover through a lack of awareness of that moment, that pain, that inability to cope. Call it loss of memory, call it coma, whatever you may wish, but it is often a way of escape so that the soul can over a period of time regain that tranquillity and peace within itself and within its material body that is so needed – it is not always a parallel world, sometimes simply a loss of consciousness or even a loss of memory if the trauma is great enough.

Q: If we stay with the analogy of the soldier who was standing next to me and disappeared, is it his entire physical body that has gone to a parallel world?

M: That is so. This is just one of those places where it is possible, it can happen. Usually it happens that another aspect of the soul enters into the personality and allows the respite, the release that the incarnating soul so greatly needs. In a way it takes over. There might perhaps be a period of lack of awareness, maybe there is unconsciousness for a period of time. Perhaps if it is happening in a hospital the return into consciousness from an operation brings with it not the incarnating soul aspect but another soul aspect from the Higher Self which is better able to cope with the trauma – to find that the life is threatened or that a limb has been severed which was not expected because the purpose of the operation was not meant to be so extensive.

Now, again, two things can occur here. The other aspect can work hand-in-hand, as it were, with the incarnating aspect so that both together have a greater strength, a greater ability to overcome and to allow as much restoration of peace and energy to gather that could not have been acquired by the one that has been traumatised. It is always the soul on behalf of its personality that endeavours to bring it through what could very well prove to be too great a trauma to allow life to continue. Or the incarnating personality can be taken to a parallel world. There it is given another existence, another body in which to live, to be aware with or without conscious memory, usually without. Usually there is another life, more incidents which are quite comfortable with the personality and which it might enjoy for a state of weeks or months or even for a longer time.

A new aspect
Meanwhile, the new aspect that has entered is left to hold the stage, you might say, a little bewildered not knowing the other characters within that play and as it meets relatives, close members of the friendship there can well be a bewilderment. Why am I fond of you, I don't feel fond of you or why do I feel I should be antagonistic to this person when there is an awareness of the soul within and therefore I feel there should be a friendship level here, not antipathy? Many, many rushes of memory, perhaps of previous lifetimes of which the other aspect

never had awareness. So there are many, many scenarios that can indeed take place when other aspects enter for the best reasons. Sometimes that aspect may remain in order to provide further learning, further awareness within the life of the teaching that is available, to heal a breach, to heal a marriage. The other aspect may return feeling they have had a wonderful dream, really recuperating and marvellous experience within the sleep state to find that the worst fears of what may have taken place indeed never happened. The other aspect knows they have and this interchange into the parallel world is the true purpose of having the parallel worlds, this is why they were created, not for the over-dramatic reasons which very occasionally occur, because they also are needed.

Q: So is the reality of the planet that they live on identical to this planet. Are the mountains in the same place for example?

M: Absolutely, it is an absolute replica.

Q: So literally it is the spirits on the Earth that are on a different vibration but not necessarily the Earth itself. Although we are adjusting our environment, they are not adjusting in the parallel world?

M: Yes, perhaps the parallel world is going through a different stage of development, it is going through this development of peace, learning through understanding, learning through discussion, through being at one with one's neighbour instead of warring with him. It is a choice when the soul first comes into life as to whether it basically chooses a reclusive life, a life of peace and harmony being rewarded for past traumas, past disciplines that have been forced upon a different aspect, in which case the whole of the life can be lead in that tranquil world of peaceful lakes, sunlit days, quiet understandings and conversations with those that share that world with it.

Q: So I assume that this is not the world that I am in, then?

M: It cannot be, can it, my son? Because we are so aware of the trauma that is taking place all around you. In different parts of the world, the Middle East at the present time and of course, although you didn't experience personally the major war fifty years ago you have been more aware of subsequent more condensed wars which have affected your life in its comfort in one way or another.

Q: So is it a single parallel world or as you have said in previous teaching there are actually three worlds concurrent? You have also said that those worlds will converge at a point as we slow down and reach a rhythm closer to the other parallel world, so we will become one world again?

M: This has indeed happened twice before. Now in the spiral of the world's activities in the past, let us take the world of Atlantis which was the last world to converge. It was a fairly tranquil existence for approximately 250,000 years and suddenly there was the introduction of quite violent disorders as some people became very greedy and wanting far more from life than others. There were those who for a very long time had been content with what the crystal energy was able to give to them and then there were those being born who wanted more than this. They wanted fame, they wanted to own, to achieve, to have. They used the opposite side of the coin to the spiritual development and they began to develop a link with the occult, with the evil that can so easily be raised within the human world. So in a way their world diverged, divided. There were those who still were processing the crystal energies for the good of man and there were those that were using it for power. Inevitably there had to come a time when one or the other would succeed in what they were manifesting.

The downfall of Atlantis
If you have not already read, we are sure you will do so, the climax of the Atlantean continent and exactly what took place and what caused it was the violent clash between good and evil. Neither could win, both were too powerful. Those that had been using the energies for the advancement of man, those that were virtually going to destroy that planet and destroy man with it, they clashed head on. It was through using the occult energies that brought up the volcano from within the adjacent mountain that looked down upon a golden palace. Already the continent had been diminishing over approximately 50,000 years, becoming smaller and smaller as the oceans encroached. By the time that Atlantis was due to finish its existence there

was a very small part of the continent left which was known as Poseidonis. We suppose it would be approximately the size of the continental countries of Belgium, France, Switzerland, Germany and so forth, that part of western Europe, with the oceans surrounding it and other land masses largely unoccupied that had already completed their existence.

An exodus
There was also another quite active continent which had always worked in harmony with Atlantis and which also was suffering the same privations and very aware of the conflict that was going on between good and evil and keeping well away from it. When they could seize their chance, the survivors of that much smaller continent, possibly the size of Britain and Ireland together, they using their crafts that they had fashioned had set sail. They arrived on a large landmass which was completely untouched by human hand. There were animals, many animals were there and man had not yet made his appearance. It was a fairly newly arisen landmass from the oceans and so the Nubian tribes began in the far north of what is now known as Egypt.

Meanwhile in Atlantis the battles between good and evil went on. When the mountain exuded its anger and its wrath and consumed large areas of the land then those who were ready for this to occur got into their crafts and set sail. Many, of course, perished in the oceans but there were those also, especially those who needed to survive, who landed in the lower reaches of Egypt through the Nile passage and on to land. There was a sudden convergence of energies, parallel worlds merged together. That which survived were those that were working for the truth, working for good, that were in more direct link with the God force and not with evil. All that was evil perished, it was a new beginning, a new start. There were the two peoples, those that were black and those that were predominately white-skinned, as they are known. So at that time there was this merging, there was this beginning again with perfection as it had been reached without evil, without the desire for power which was eventually once more sowing its seeds between the Nubians and the Egyptians who were, as we say, the descendants of the Atlanteans. Now this is a very brief synopsis of what occurred.

Q: That explains the variation in age between so many of the ancient objects found in Egypt for which science has not yet come up with an explanation.

M: Absolutely, and gradually many things are being pieced together. For example, those studying the religious books, especially those of the Bible, have realised that if you only take the timescale in the Old Testament as a guideline of when things occurred that it was indeed ten to twelve thousand years ago that this calamity occurred with Atlantis and coincides with Noah's flood. So you have got some of those in their craft with their animals that were epitomised by Noah's family and his seeking land, seeking a place in which to allow these creatures to live. Many of those were, of course, the half-man, half-animal creatures that assisted the Atlanteans so much within their work with crystal energy and with helping people to survive, to overcome hideous illnesses. They had a Utopia, they had a life that man today craves, is endeavouring through science once more to bring forth and to achieve.

Q: Is that driven by the Higher Self's knowledge that that existence can be reached again?

M: Indeed, indeed.

Q: But what we are doing here is raping and destroying our planet in order to achieve it.

M: That again is the negative force, we prefer the word negative to that of evil, positive – negative, which is reflected in absolutely everything.

Q: But then so many people are coming to populate this Earth, so many souls have chosen to experience the destruction of this style of life that that is a self-fulfilling prophecy. If so many come and strive to achieve and know they are actually coming to experience its end then its end is an inevitability which must already be mapped out. So that must be therefore the convergence of the two parallel worlds?

M: Indeed, but do bear this in mind – the end of something must be the beginning of what arises from it. There can be no absolute annihilation, there can be no complete death. There is always something which transforms, which again bursts forth into life, new purpose, new creation, new understanding where the souls once more can congregate, can use their free will.

Q: That will be why the Children of Light are here.

M: Indeed.

Q: Are you saying that it is only the Children of Light that will survive?

M: There will be others. There will be those who are being born and continue to be born for a long while yet who will be helping them. But there will be also those more negative beings who will survive that they may continue to learn the difference between good and evil, between the positive and the negative aspect of all things. Nothing can just disintegrate and not be.

Q: I can accept that. As the two parallel worlds converge and have done in the past, was there a parallel world during the Atlantean time that did not have the same conflict as the Atlantean world was experiencing?

M: There were the two worlds. There was the relative peace and harmony and love which was in the crystal aspect of Atlantis which you might say would represent the positive, and there was the parallel world where power was the main objective. Where there was still crystal, there was still all the energy that was needed, but the humanity in that world was struggling for the power. Struggling to overcome in order that their existence might give more and more.

Q: Then the world that was the tranquil world, the positive world, was that world aware that the more negative world was going to be partly its downfall as well?

M: On a purely spiritual level of understanding the consciousness of the world, of the Earth, does provide that knowledge, yes. Not so much with humanity – they are too preoccupied with their everyday learning, their everyday being, but the actual Earth is aware of its parallel, is aware of what is taking place. Because on a vibrational level it is part of the plan, part of that which the Creator envisioned for the knowledge of good and evil, the acceptance of what can be attained by using one power and what can be attained or maybe lost through using another. Is it becoming clearer, my son?

Q: So the intelligence that is the Earth is controlling the activities around it and the energies upon it by allowing the parallel worlds to exist and then using that manipulation to ensure that the correct force moves forward. So the destruction of one form of Atlantis was to give birth to our current existence, to allow us to start again to see if we could get it right this time. Is that right?

M: That is so. So Lemuria which gave rise to the Nubians and Atlantis which gave rise to the Egyptians was an intended progress pattern for the Earth or the Earth's at that particular moment in time. The convergence had to be, it was part of the world's existence levels.

Q: So the next convergence is an inevitability. When will it be?

M: Sometime in the future, quite honestly we don't know exactly when. It all depends so much on the actions of man. If, for example, there is another nuclear war and that happened in a few months' time then it would accelerate everything to a very great extent.

Q: So it really is at the behest of the consciousness or the intelligence of the Earth that will dictate.

M: Indeed so. It was averted at the end of the last world war through the good vibrations asserting themselves and the victory from those who were not power hungry, power crazy, that averted the nuclear war which would have laid the Earth waste except possibly for a continent such as Australia or South Africa which would have only had a very small part of the fall-out, enough probably to survive and mankind there to continue to proceed with the everyday purpose of living and growing. But it didn't happen, it was averted, the power of good over evil is virtually always manifest.

Q: I understand that there is life on other planets, but it might not be a life that we can see.

M: Exactly, it is a different vibrational rate. People often laugh at the TV series that is watched by so many millions which is to do with interplanetary travel. But it is a possibility, maybe a thousand years into the future, if science takes another leap forward and manages to navigate through the boundaries of these energies between the planets and the Earth and discovers the means whereby man can indeed survive in different atmospheres. Again we are not in the way of prediction, but all things are possible. Nothing is impossible, nothing is irreversible either. All things that occurred throughout the experience of man can reoccur and they can also give rise to a different motivation, a different way forward. Imagine if the other side had won the last war instead of the western world having control and starting a more realistic and peaceful way of life. Supposing it had been the other way? Supposing the whole world came under the possession of a dictatorship? It could have happened, if it did happen life would still have gone forward but in a very different way. Because it was different nations that won the peace, nations that didn't wish to participate, nations that were not after that kind of power the world has gone forward to its particular time now.

The third parallel world
There is a parallel world, the third one of which we spoke, where those energies that nearly succeeded did succeed and so the world of domination, the world of excess, the world of fear continued for a very long while, possibly into thirty or forty years after the last war. Then there was violation, then there was the integration and there was the extermination, you might say; that particular life force no longer exists.

Q: So the Earth destroyed an entire parallel world because ...?

M: Indeed, because there were no boundaries, no good and evil, no positive and negative. So it could not exist within itself.

Q: But that parallel world can only be a slight adjustment in a vibration from this world and yet it can suffer such a trauma without this world knowing?

M: Indeed. So you see, my son, it is a very vast subject and it could go on for a long while. We are also realising that we are approaching the end of our time with you. So if there is any point within the discussion that needs clarification before we finish with this subject, perhaps you could present it to us.

Q: You said that the last convergence of parallel worlds was only twelve thousand years ago. Then there was a volcanic eruption that destroyed Atlantis and ended the Atlantean Age. Why isn't it seen, why is it so hidden and not understood by scientists because it is comparatively not that long ago?

M: No, we would say they probably have viewed it, looked into it and not thought that it was of any particular moment because they still do not accept the existence of Atlantis. They accept an existence of continents, of things that happened to those continents, of the fact that most of the Earth disappeared in rushes of waters that swelled the oceans. All of this they accept and as there were many explosions within the mountains but not all at the same time, it was only the one that was adjacent to Poseidonis that actually gave rise to that part of the continent being destroyed. More and more investigation is being done underwater, in the rock face, at the bottom of the ocean and it is there that science is beginning to accept, to understand that there are things that can be proved to which they have not yet given due thought and the preparation of their investigations sufficiently.

Questions and Answers on Soul

This section is made up of individual paragraphs from trances given over the last ten years. Some were in response to questions and some were spoken by the Teachers in the course of discourses on other subjects. They are gathered here under subject headings but are not necessarily sequential.

Incarnation

The moment when the soul decides it wishes to progress in a way that it has not hitherto progressed is traumatic. It has, up to the moment of conception, known only those environments which hold it close as an embryo of love, peaceful with itself, understanding of spirit life; but it knows that in order to become complete it must face the rigours and the hardships of the earthly life. There are many homes for the soul and the Earth is but one facet. There are many facets within the soul itself and each has to know and understand the Earth life. Until each part has been conceived and born and lived, it is not complete. We heard it described once by a learned one who was upon the plane of Earth, that the soul can be likened to the parts of an orange. When the orange is complete with the skin around the fruit, the soul is complete. Then, as the orange is peeled and each piece is removed from the whole and then replaced again, it is the same and yet different. It is the same because each piece has been replaced together, but it is different because the outer covering which has concealed all knowledge and understanding has been removed and in removing it, the knowledge and understanding enter into it, as would the juice of the fruit, spreading through each piece, blending understanding in each facet.

The lives of man

The soul is not always understood by even those who have studied greatly and who have had many, many lifetimes upon the Earth plane, that the meaning of life, eternal life, is locked within that which is known as the soul. The soul is a wonderful instrument. It was designed and created by a mind which defies all understanding. When thinking man looks upon the world as it is at the present time, he wonders that there could be such a wonderful creative mind behind such seeming chaos; and yet it was this very free will which was created with the idea of progress, of the wonderment of the universe being unfolded before all mankind as the ages roll on. This marvellous gift of decision has in itself been instrumental in destroying the very seeds of understanding and truth which it was meant to create.

Man has lived through countless ages. Man has moved through time and space, enjoying within himself the creations of the time in which he lived, strong within himself, whatever knowledge and understanding was attained by his particular mind and brain during any given lifetime. At the end of each life there was a return again to the spirit spheres, in order to be able to understand that every moment of that existence had created its own karmic pattern, stored within the Akashic Record. Each moment of the lifetime is there recorded; each act, be it one of glory or one of deceit; each thought which has left the mind, perpetrated by the brain within the human being, has reached its own particular life recorded therein. It is this automatic action which occurs from the moment that life is given breath which creates the karma through which you are living at the present time. Those who believe they live but once have no understanding of the mind behind the brain which created life.

The etheric body
The personality which encompasses your soul at the present time has but one existence, one lifetime. It is this personality which initially returns to the spirit realms in order to gain for itself the whole idea of the meaning behind that one life. The personality returns in what is known as the etheric body – the perfect counterpart of the physical which you are wearing now; and when the time eventually arrives that this etheric counterpart is no longer required, then and only then it will disintegrate within the map of time and will be no more but an echo of what has passed, what has lived and been recorded. It can be blown away as a speck of dust within the atmosphere of Earth; but the soul – what is the soul ?

The soul emanates from all that is spirit, all that is life. The soul is an individual particle of thought and the soul will, for countless millions of years, journey through space and light and understanding, until it then decides that it will incarnate in a body upon the plane of Earth. Why Earth? Why not Pluto? Why not Jupiter? Earth was specially created from the mind of the Creator – He who you wish to call God– especially that the incarnating soul can learn for itself the lessons which it can only receive through having a physical human body.

Elsewhere within the universe, conditions are so perfect, so co-ordinated explicitly within this mind, that there is only knowledge and understanding and truth. There is no one and nothing that can interfere with that perfection, therefore there had to be a part of the universe set aside that the soul may understand the meaning behind the idea of creation. It is upon your plane of Earth that you can make mistakes and then correct them, that you can make decisions regarding the life and death of your fellow man and he in you. It is within this wonderful plane – the desire plane – where you can create your own life and you can draw within yourselves the knowledge and understanding of that which is spiritual. Your soul can expand its knowledge and it can then move forward – outward upon the plane of life, to give this knowledge and understanding to others who have not yet reached that peak of living, that absorption which those who have returned time and time again have reached within themselves.

Many lifetimes
You not only have many lifetimes, you are able to choose for yourselves when you will come to this Earth and when you will return to the spirit realm which you have made for yourself during that lifetime. You can turn your back on all things spiritual; you can move only within the circles which form the desire and the lust of the body; you can initially take on the form of primitive man, moving within the same lifetime in the form of the advanced man, drawing from within yourself all knowledge and understanding of truth, for it is all there. You have only to look within to seek the light and you will be dazzled by the truth which is shown to you. The lessons that you learn here upon this plane of Earth are hard ones. They are intended to be. If they were not difficult, you would not be here, you would have descended in the form of man and returned upon the instant of being born, if you had not already decided within yourself which way you will be treading and what your lesson will be; and having once set foot upon this pathway, there is no looking back.

The Masters and Teachers who are upon the plane of knowledge are near enough to commune with your earthly minds, to look within that which is known as the brain and to help to stimulate the desire for knowledge. You can close your ears, you can refuse to listen, but at some time within this particular incarnation, you will be forced to unveil your eyes and open your ears, for that which it is intended that you should learn about will present itself again and again. You have all been born at a wonderful time of dawning knowledge and understanding. It has been referred to in many circles as the dawning of the Aquarian Age, the age when that which is mind will perpetuate and expand, that all knowledge will be available for you to look upon. It is the now which matters to your soul, not the past, not that which is contained in the future, for there is no future, there is only the now. So it was and so it will be for ever more, that this instant in time is all that exists and you can shape that instant within yourself.

Connecting with the soul

Those who have studied and practised meditation are aware of the benefits of being able to raise their consciousness above the level of mundane things of everyday living. It is difficult to do this if there is no knowledge within the human regarding the relationship between the physical and spiritual, the spiritual being the soul body and the physical being the human personality of this incarnation. Let us assume that the soul has been born – born in space, born from a burst of energy, millions and billions of years before – and as the particles separate and become individual, so they are born in a physical body upon the plane of Earth; but although each particle is individual and contains within itself a mind, a memory, it also contains collectively the energising spirit of life, without which there is no function, and this spirit we term intelligence. When intelligence leaves the body in all its forms, then the physical body no longer lives, but the important part, the etheric, or the counterpart enveloping the soul, continues to live in another dimension, another time.

Some find it difficult to imagine another world, a world which is part of this one, which exists within it and around it, but because of its change of vibration, is not visible to the eye of the human being; and yet this world is perfection itself. All things upon your Earth world emanate from it. There is nothing which you have which does not have its counterpart within these spheres, and the minds who invent some of your wonders, invent them from the knowledge that has already existed within those spheres. There are many spheres. There is the sphere where all ideas and inventions emerge from; there are the Halls of Learning, there are the Temples of Healing; and if you should see those particular Temples, you would be able to meditate upon them for the rest of your life.

Everlasting life

You have, within the physical body which is yours, only two essential parts to everlasting life – your spirit and your mind. The mind is indestructible, the mind goes on through infinite time. Aspects of the mind return within each new body, as each reincarnation is commenced upon. The spirit which animates your soul is also everlasting and it is the mind, animated by this spirit, which is individually yours, which gives function to the soul – your spiritual self. Initially, those who enter into the spirit realms are able to distinguish one from another with that which is called the etheric self – the counterpart of the body you are holding now – but after a period of time this etheric self ceases to be. We cannot give you any specific time span, for time in the spirit realms is not measured as it is upon the earthly plane. The now, for the etheric body, can be many, many years of earthly time. It is a time of adjustment, it is a time of realisation of what has, or has not, been learnt while in the earthly body. Once this realisation has been accepted, the soul can then travel, it can expand into the higher realms from whence it can go on and on into infinity. During the period of the now, it is possible to decide to return to the Earth, or to some other sphere of life, in order to continue the expansion and the realisation of the meaning of existence.

Why are we here?

So why are you here? If, apparently, this earthly existence does not even scratch the surface of the understanding of life's meaning, why come here in the first instance and why return, possibly again and again, through centuries of time, if it has no meaning? There is indeed a meaning to this earthly life. Many lessons must be learnt and one of the main lessons for all human beings, distinguishing them from inanimate life, from animal life and from plant life is that you must always bare the open mind to that which is new. If you look back into the realms of history, even the history of the last one hundred years, you will see the birth of many things. This last century of your time has seen the birth of electric power, it has seen the conquest, first of the heavens, then of the planets. It has seen the extinction also of things which were considered everyday occurrences 150-170 years ago. Where in the modern world will you now find a train propelled by steam, except as some historic land-mark in a museum, on a specially laid railway track? Even in the less forward countries of the world, steam is a rarity. The electric power and, in some cases, atomic power, is now used. Very often it needs some earthly tragedy to enable the scientific minds to perfect some new and essential part of life's creation. Atomic power was brought to the front in the last of your World Wars and is now being used, not predominantly for destruction, but for the help and the formation of mankind. It is due to these ages, these ages of setback and progress alternately, which enables humankind to see clearly the meaning behind existence.

The human mind
Those who are, to this very day, teaching from the spirit realms, through such as my own medium, find the frailty of the human mind a setback when it comes to trying to place before them the wonder of the true world. The mind has inexhaustible pos-sibilities. If you can relax totally and put from you the harass-ment of the day, allow some of the visions from those in spirit to be set before your inner vision, you would be able also to form your pathway according to the directions set when you were still but spirit beings yourselves. The lives of all of you, spent both severally and independently before you were born into earthly bodies, was spent according to strict rules. The pathway was clear before you and always that very special dawning of light granted you, helped and inspired you; but when the earthly incarnations began, this particular light was shielded from your sight, for it would be too blinding to one who had no knowledge or concept initially, in the infant guise and body. As all infants must learn from the example of others and from their own mistakes, so, too, must those on the pathway of life learn from the mistakes they make within the life. The tenuous thread which holds the soul within the human frame can be transcended in the state of sleep and you can mingle with those who have gone before you, as well as those who are there to help and inspire and guide you; and if your minds are thus attuned, the realisation, when waking, can remain with you. If it were not for the stress of the day, the anx-

ieties which flood in from the moment of awakening, if you could gently allow yourself to come back from these realms, to re-inhabit your earthly body with gentleness and to ponder upon that which has been set before you during your sleep state, you would be more refreshed for the start of the day.

The stress of living

The tumultuous efforts of trying to contend with earthly conditions, is trying for the soul. The soul desires to be free, but mankind has put himself into enormous buildings where the smells of nature are excluded. The very air which man breathes has the pollution of the years, and the life blood which circulates in the veins is tainted with disease.

It is so difficult for even those with the most aspiring natures to be able to cast themselves into the future and to understand that which is expected of them, when they have to cope with an environment such as is surrounding you at this time. Those who live in other areas of the world, such as the area which you refer to as the Himalayas, find it so much easier to communicate with their inner selves and with the Cosmic Intelligence, for they have surrounding them the purity and the beauty of the things which nature intended man to imbibe within himself.

Do not always look upon that which appears to destroy as being the end of life. It is not the end of anything; it is but the beginning of something new. As the chrysalis becomes the butterfly, so, too, does the ugliest of the creation of man turn into the beauty and radiance of the soul.

New birth

The initial transition from man to spirit can also be ugly. All forms of death are not beautiful. The human eye can behold the most appalling of tragedies to the human frame, but once life is extinct within that frame, the new birth opens up into the butterfly. It opens its wings, it flies away and it is reborn and renewed within itself. All that which has gone on through the life is kept within the mind. The mind has no confines; although this is a favourite saying of many, the confines of the mind do not exist. It can expand to infinite proportions, creating and recreating within itself all concepts of all forms of life through the ages.

Nothing is wasted

All of you were born from spirit, all of you have known many lifetimes, many ages. Many of you have descended from the Age of Capricorn and during that particular age, many of you reached heights of understanding which you would never dream of within the bodies you now inhabit, but that knowledge and understanding was not wasted when you returned once more to the Earth. You may have returned in humbler stature, but the knowledge that you have attained has made the complete whole, which when it is established, will be laid before you and the understanding will be yours to look upon.

The Higher Self, Soul and Reincarnation

Initially soul was one vast energy field. At a particular point in evolution this exploded into a myriad of particles which gathered together into Higher Selves. The Master has often said that it is difficult to explain the true nature of the Higher Self. Language itself is based on what individuals see around them and it is difficult to understand what cannot be perceived.

Each individual soul is an aspect or particle of a Higher Self and each Higher Self contains more particles than there are cells in a human body. Not all aspects incarnate, just as a woman has the potential to conceive hundreds of children in a lifetime but may only actually give birth to two or three children. At the end of life the individualised soul returns to the Higher Self and the experiences and learning of that life is shared throughout the entire Higher Self. Once an aspect has incarnated it cannot return; each aspect or cell of the Higher Self can only incarnate once. Because of this, when a soul returns, something akin to a conference takes place where the karma is reviewed, the experiences and understanding of life are evaluated and a new aspect steps forward, with the essence of the previous life within, to take the learning forward.

If the Higher Self could be seen, it would resemble a vast rainbow, the particles that comprise it are organized according to the colours of that rainbow, called light streams – pink, amethyst, gold, silver, green and blue and all the hundreds of shades in between. Each light stream has a different learning pattern and this pattern typically takes two to three hundred incarnations to fulfil, also each Higher Self has an average of over one thousand light streams within it. The Master defined a light stream in the following way:

'A light stream, or directional light particle, is an impulse of combined energy factors which permit the soul to choose and travel along a particular path of endeavour towards enlightenment. It is that which gives the ability for attainment mentally and intellectually while the soul is in the limited confines of matter.'

The Higher Self can incarnate more than one individualised soul at a time. Often in the later stages of spiritual development these souls that share a Higher Self incarnate as members of the same family.

Apparently if one could view the Higher Self one would be delighted by its great beauty. The Master has said:

'Imagine looking at a sunset, how the sky above radiates the light, how each cloud represents a facet of the pinks and oranges, the blues and greens of the sunset; and then imagine the Higher Self.

'Some may say, 'But if the soul has such proportions how is there room for so many in spirit?' But spirit is not measured by an area of space; spirit is a dimension. It is not like your world where you must travel from one place to another in order to experience the change of view, the different countries and the people dwelling in them. Spirit being a dimension of light contains all things in a relatively small area in comparison with your world. Unfortunately, to be able to visualise that which you have never seen is virtually impossible.'

So a true insight into the Higher Self – the total soul – can never be achieved because it is of a vastly different vibration from that of which the body is aware.

The soul has the opportunity to learn in spirit as well as upon the Earth, but the earth is an important school for the soul, where the Higher Self can enrich its understanding with first-hand knowledge of the full range of human emotions. Ultimately it is where the Higher Self can come to know love. It is the planet where the soul can express itself, can move forward and has that greatest blessing of all – free will. The soul in its own environment does not have free will. It has total knowledge and understanding of life and universal law; it has accepted what it is simply to be, but that is not sufficient for truly understanding the lessons that life can offer, lessons such as compassion, tolerance, understanding and patience.

When the soul enters the physical self at the time of birth, conscious knowledge of the past is concealed. Later, at different times of life, an aspect of the Higher Self that has lived before and that has an interest or karmic investment in the particular events or lessons that are being lived through will step forward to offer help, assistance and understanding. This help is often initially recognized through synchronicity, experiences of *déjà vu* or dreaming. Through meditation and spiritual development such a link with a 'spirit guide' can be built upon and parts of the past life can even be recalled. The spiritually enhanced understanding of the guide can then help the individual to go forward, develop and succeed.

The single cell principle

The first cell within the universe resonated a sound throughout space and that sound also proclaimed itself as light, growing brighter and clearer and vaster as it was carried on the wings of sound until the whole universe was one glowing vibration of light. The atom is like this – it grows from one minute point, one cell, and it grows so rapidly, continuously breaking within itself, and each cell of that unit doubles and triples and quadruples until again it is as vast as the original cell. It keeps moving in this fashion until the rays of light and energy which flow from it are stabilised and are again broken into various parts. Initially these became the planetary life of which Earth is a part. So all things, whatever they may be, from the smallest to the greatest, start from one cell.

There is memory within the cell as to how the individual is to be, how the animal, plant and mineral life are to be, so that they are well represented and the pattern can be repeated without any thought of change – a blueprint for life. One cell within the body knows that it will always be an elbow, a knee or a foot; that when it has ceased to multiply it will be formed into this perfect part. It is one of the miracles which surrounds mankind, this DNA, this memory pattern within the cell.

The individual seed from which mankind grows is of course individual within each body. It is that seed which is fertilised within the womb and which grows into the foetus, the child. It multiplies constantly and within that multiplication it develops into the human being whose personality it is throughout that life. There is an important factor within that seed – because it is the first single seed of life it also represents that first seed of life from which all life first formed, therefore when there is sickness or illness of any kind, if that particular seed is visualised, it represents holistic healing and health within the self.

It is not easy to imagine a single cell – almost impossible to do so – so we suggest that a symbol is used, usually that of a star or a sun or a moon, anything which represents life, progress and wholeness, then when doing your absent healing for others or your own self-healing because of some malady, you imagine this symbol and send the healing within it, radiating truth and love and wholeness.